Tears of Faith

From Life's Storms into God's Miracles

Sheila McDaniel

This work reflects actual events in the life of the author as truthfully as recollection permits. Some events have been compressed, and some dialogue has been recreated. While all persons within are actual individuals, names and identifying characteristics have been changed to protect their privacy.

Copyright 2025 by Sheila McDaniel

All rights reserved. No part of this book may be reproduced or used in any manner without written permission of the copyright owner except for the use of quotations in a book review.

For more information,
Email address: mcdanielsheila@gmail.com

Ebook ISBN: 979-8-9926314-1-8
Hardcover ISBN: 979-8-9926314-0-1

Dedication

To the strong, tenacious, courageous overcomers, and survivors who draw their strength from the One and Only Living God—you are the embodiment of faith in action. Look toward the Heavens with praises to our Lord and Savior, Jesus Christ, for through Him, all things are made possible. You were uniquely created, filled with courage, goodness, success, and the divine power to overcome any challenge that stands before you. Remember always who you are: a cherished child of God, created for greatness, destined to leave an indelible mark on this world through your unwavering faith and perseverance.

Foreword

In a world where hope often seems distant and trials feel insurmountable, Sheila McDaniel's "Tears of Faith" emerges as a beacon of light, illuminating the path through life's darkest valleys. This remarkable memoir isn't just another story of perseverance—it's a raw and powerful testament to the transformative power of unwavering faith.

As you turn these pages, you'll walk alongside Sheila through moments that would have broken many spirits: devastating setbacks, profound losses, and challenges that seemed designed to destroy her very foundation. Yet, through each trial, through every tear shed, Sheila reveals how faith became not just her anchor, but her compass.

What makes this narrative extraordinary isn't just the obstacles Sheila faced, but how she transmuted her pain into purpose. Her story reminds us that our greatest difficulties often precede our most significant breakthroughs. Through her experiences, we learn that tears aren't always symbols of defeat—sometimes they're the water that nourishes the seeds of our future victories. This book isn't merely about survival; it's about God's divine intervention in the midst of natural impossibilities. Sheila's accounts of miracles aren't distant, theoretical concepts, but tangible testimonies that will challenge your perspective on what's possible when faith enters the equation.

As you embark on this journey through "Tears of Faith," prepare to be more than just moved—prepare to be transformed. Sheila's story will remind you that your current chapter isn't your conclusion, that your tears can water the garden of your future testimony, and that faith, even as small as a mustard seed, can indeed move mountains.

Whether you're standing in the valley of decision, climbing your own mountain of challenges, or seeking reassurance that miracles still happen, this book holds a message for you. Sheila's journey from devastation to victory offers more than inspiration—it provides a blueprint for maintaining faith when everything around you suggests otherwise.

Welcome to a story that will change how you view your own trials and triumphs. Welcome to "Tears of Faith."

-Dr. Perdita Meeks

Table Of Contents

Introduction 1

Chapter 1: Your Past Doesn't Define Your Future 9

Chapter 2: It's Okay To Start Over At Any Age And Stage Of Your Life .. 29

Chapter 3: God Is Omnipresent - Talk To Him Often - At Any Time 53

Chapter 4: Developing A Relationship With God 83

Chapter 5: Your Heart's Desires Come With Faith Challenges 97

About The Author 115

Introduction

From the age of seven, I grew up in a single parent household with two of my three sisters. My mother's family was Baptist and my father's family was Pentecostal, therefore I was exposed to a Christian environment at an early age. However, I didn't attend church until I visited both grandparents in Alabama during the summers. A few weeks before my 30th birthday, I realized my life was changing when I lost the urge to go clubbing with girlfriends at the Tarsus club until it closed, then head to the after-hours motorcycle club. I had no desire to date or engage in romantic encounters any longer. It was like those party flames died overnight without any warning. After the smoke from the death of the flames subsided, I saw my path to the church. Since then, I've attended church regularly. As a single parent I knew it was time to build a strong spiritual foundation for my son, Paul who was about 6 years old at the time. I started attending Sunday school and regular services each week. As I continually attended church, I began to read the Bible more regularly and developed a desire to learn more about the word of God.

You're probably wondering what happened in my life that made those desires fade. Well, I'm glad you asked. One night, I had a dream. An illuminated hand reached down from the sky, and a gentle voice said, "Sheila, it's time." At that moment, I knew it was God's hand, and I understood what He meant. The Lord was telling me that it was time to stop running from the call, my inner feeling, and to surrender my life to Him. I was instructed to live a more spiritual life while helping others along the way.

I always thought I'd surrender eventually, but only after I'd had my share of partying and fun. I always thought being a Christian was boring, but that wasn't true. Through my relationship with God, I discovered that when I focused on Him and not on tradition, my relationship with Him became uniquely fulfilling.

There is a verse in the Bible that says "Death and life *are* in the power of the tongue, And those who love it will eat its fruit" (Proverbs 18:21). This means speaking positivity over a situation can create life in that circumstance. I would tell God, "I believe You will bless my finances, and when I go to the mailbox there will be a check for me." Well, there wasn't a check but there was cash–a crisp $1 bill in an envelope from a company that I had never heard of. God heard me and did increase my finances but I wasn't specific with my ask so I shouldn't have expected much. That was so comical, and touched my funny bone as I giggled all the way back inside, saying, "God, You got me." That's when I learned that God has a sense of humor.

This was an indication that my life would be interesting, amusing, unpredictable and extraordinary.

Over the next few weeks, I tried to understand how I would function in a Christian environment. I knew I wouldn't be a traditional, Bible-thumping Christian because that wasn't my personality. I knew the change from the way I was living would be a continual growing process to get to where I thought The Lord wanted me to be.

The first step in my walk with God was accepting that He didn't make a mistake when He called me to serve Him. The second step was to step away from my partying lifestyle. The third step was finding the strength to stand up to Christians who expected me to live a "holier than thou" lifestyle. Meaning, one where I did no wrong, criticized others, walked on water, refused to speak to others in everyday English, but quoted scriptures from the Bible constantly.

On October 2nd, 1993, during a revival in Cherry Hill, New Jersey, I said, "YES" to the Lord and my life changed forever. I remember it like it was yesterday. I was dressed super cute, in a cobalt blue silk long-sleeve sheath dress that reached mid-thigh with nearly three inches of large pleats at the bottom, black patent leather heels, smelling delicious, and my hair long and full of body. The choir was singing, "Someone prayed for me," with a gentle Caribbean beat beneath each word. Elder Mann asked everyone to stand as he made an altar call, inviting anyone in the congregation to give their life to Christ.

Although I had already felt God's reach in my dream, an internal battle raged within me as I watched others stand and walk to the front. Was I ready to commit? One of my closest friends, Debbie, stood next to me with her hands out and her head bowed. I looked up at her and lightly grabbed her left hand, tight, almost as if she was anchoring me to where I was standing. When I let go of her hand, I grabbed the back of the chair in front of me. I gripped the back of that chair with both hands, my body twisting from side to side, overwhelmed by the Holy Spirit. Before I knew it, my hold was released and I was walking down the aisle with my hands raised, tears streaming down my cheek.

I remember seeing Pastor Daymon, his wife, and other members of the Church of God by Faith, stand as I slowly walked down the aisle. They rose to their feet, knowing my past life was behind me. They understood that from that day forward, nothing would ever be the same. When I arrived at the front of the room, I hugged Elder Mann and wept in his chest. Elder Mann was an older husky gentleman. He had never met me before that moment, and it was a no-no to hug a man in church. I was overcome with emotion, my hug was strictly an emotional reaction. One of a grandfather hugging his granddaughter.

To be honest, I don't remember if there were others at the altar with me. At that moment, it was just me.

After reciting the sinner's prayer out loud (Romans 10:9-10), I wiped away my tears, gathered my composure, turned around to face the congregation, and confidently walked back to my seat.

> Romans 10:9-10 (NKJV)
> [9] If you declare with your mouth, "Jesus is Lord," and believe in your heart that God raised Him from the dead, you will be saved.
> [10] For it is with your heart that you believe and are justified, and it is with your mouth that you profess your faith and are saved.

My life was changed that day, and I've never regretted my decision. But that's the thing, we all have a choice to make: Do we want to walk this path alone, or do we want to rest in our Father's arms and seek His wisdom? I was tired of the consequences of my old ways. I needed to experience something new. The Christian journey has not been without challenges, every day brought and continues to bring new obstacles. But knowing that at the end of my earthly life, I will be in Heaven with Christ for eternity is a promise I'm committed to.

In my book, *Tears of Faith*, you will understand how God uniquely and purposely created you for this pilgrimage and the benefits of this spiritual journey.

In 2002, the Lord put it on my heart to write a book to help His people. I resisted. I was overwhelmed with life, my marriage had failed, I was struggling to hold it together for my children, and the idea of writing a book felt impossible. I cried out, "Lord, I can't do this right now. I'm barely keeping it together. I don't have the strength to add one more thing to my plate." *Nope, I'm not going to write a book at this time. My main focus is my children.*

Then, in 2003, I attended another revival. Prophet Roger DeCuir entered late and headed directly to the pulpit. After the opening prayer, he stepped down from the pulpit. He walked directly to me and said, "God sent me here for you. You're the reason I'm here. I was going to cancel, but God wouldn't let me. You're the reason I'm here." As he turned to walk away. I stared at him with no expression, thinking, "If God really sent you here for me, He told you to leave that woman alone because she's not the type that is seeking a Word of prophecy from anyone."

As I finished my thought, Prophet DeCuir turned and faced me again and said, "I know you don't like people to prophesy over you, but God says you're going to write a book that will help His people before you die." I could feel the stares from everyone around me, but I didn't lose my outward composure. Inside, the words hit me like a ton of bricks. I didn't acknowledge him publicly because I knew it was God confirming what He had already spoken to my heart. I wasn't ready to write the book, but I knew it was coming.

TEARS OF FAITH

In September 2017, God gave me the title of the book: *Tears of Faith*. Still, I procrastinated, unsure about the scriptures I should include and overwhelmed by the "what-ifs." What if no one buys it? What if I don't have my PhD by the time it's done? In my mind, I thought a PhD would make the book more legitimate.

In July 2023, I took a solo 7-day Hawaiian cruise. I loved every moment. During my intimate prayer time, watching the sun rise and set, over the majestic blue ocean, listening to the waves, I felt a profound sense of peace. It was then that I began to write *Tears of Faith*.

As this book neared publication, fear and doubt crept in. I worried about family reactions and sharing painful secrets. I thought about how one of my sisters wasn't speaking to me because I shared a family tragedy from my past. Standing in the middle of my bedroom, with my hands on my hip, I looked up to Heaven and said, "Lord, I know that You have given me this mission, and under no circumstances will I let the devil try to deter, hinder, or delay me from writing this book."

By the time you reach the last page of *Tears of Faith*, you will understand that the failed relationships, loneliness, abuse, uncertainty, and disappointments were not all in vain. You will know, without any doubt, that you are a survivor. You have inner strength and determination you never knew existed. When you reach the mountaintop and look back, you'll realize: *I didn't think I could make it, but God carried me when I was too weak to walk. He was there, wiping my tears and holding my hand during my lowest moments.*

God created you with tenacity, beauty, intelligence, and the ability to accomplish anything you set your mind to. As 2 Corinthians 13:9 says, "For we are glad when we are weak and you are strong. And this also we pray, that you may be made complete."

As Isaiah 25:8 promises, "Your tears are not wasted, for God knows every tear that you shed and the Lord God will wipe away tears from all faces." And in Psalm 126:5, "You are not alone, Those who sow in tears shall reap in joy."

Yes, challenges will come. Hold your head up, lift your eyes to Heaven, stand on faith, and know that failure is not in your DNA.

CHAPTER 1

Your Past Doesn't Define Your Future

God doesn't hold our past against us. Instead, He takes the horrible experiences we've endured and transforms them, using them to help others. In the process of doing so, He gets the glory and praise.

My parents separated when I was seven years old. Some of the memories that resurface time and time again are witnessing the abusive relationship between my father and mother. I can still hear her piercing screams begging for him to stop beating her. She had a pleading shriek that, even now, brings tears to my eyes. The louder she begged for mercy, the harder he punched. As he was brutally beating her, she kept calling his name, "William, please stop. Please don't hit me. Please stop." Once he grew tired of striking her, she would sob for what seemed like hours.

When I was seven, my mother gathered up the courage to flee in the middle of the night with my sisters and me while my father was at work. Even though he'd painfully beat her like an animal, I still loved him. I remember him teaching me the Lord's prayer from an early age and gifting me a cowgirl outfit on Christmas. Somehow, I blocked out the memories of him brutally abusing my mom.

My mother became pregnant at 15, and I was born when she was 16. My father was enlisted in the army when he found out.

Back then, it was a shame for a young lady to become pregnant out of wedlock. She had to drop out of school in the tenth grade and couldn't continue her education. As a teenager, she told me how her father, my grandfather, beat her until he got tired, all because she was pregnant.

When my father left the army, he moved my mother to Torrington, Connecticut, and then to Albany, New York. That's when she found the courage to flee. To be perfectly honest, I can't recall a time when I saw them laughing or enjoying each other's company. I just remember that my mother was always nervous, timid, and afraid.

That was my version of a fairy tale. But in reality, he never took care of his daughters financially. When I was eight, he sent three red furry coats to our home, one for each of us. After we fled in the middle of the night, I never saw or spoke to him. But when I was 13, he started communicating with my mother again. I'm not sure what changed.

The summer of my 14th birthday, my sisters and I went to visit him in Torrington, for a couple of weeks. I thought my fairy tale was finally coming true; I would finally get a chance to rebuild a relationship with my daddy. I hoped we'd reconnect as if we had never left. But that dream quickly shattered as I faced a nightmare that would haunt me for decades to come. My two sisters went back to Detroit, but I chose to stay with him and his girlfriend, Diane, and her two sons.

During my extended stay with my daddy, I attended Torrington High School as a freshman. Everything was great for about a month. We were finally together. I dreamed of us trying to make up for the time we were apart. I made new friends, it seemed like everyone in that small town knew him. The chief of police was one of his closest friends—to me, that was a big deal. It meant he was now a good man.

Soon after, Diane moved out but I didn't know why. I got the feeling that she didn't care for me although I was always respectful towards her. For some reason, when my daddy wasn't around she didn't talk to me, so I would opt to stay in my room.

About a week before she left, I could hear them arguing softly in the room next to mine a couple of times. One day, I came home from school and the boys' room was empty—no bunk beds and no clothes in their closet. I didn't dare look in their bedroom as that would have been disrespectful. I waited until my daddy came home and asked him where Diane and the boys were. He simply said she left and would not be coming back. One night, I was asleep in my room when he got in the bed with me. He slithered his body under the sheets and pressed his face against the nape of my neck. I felt his warm breath graze my skin. This was not part of our normal routine. Typically, when we said goodnight, I'd venture off in my bedroom to curl up with a book and he'd stay behind watching TV in the living room until he fell asleep.

I pretended to be asleep trying to process why he wasn't in his own bed. The next thing I knew, he was holding me down, with his hand over my mouth, and whispering in a low raspy voice, "Don't say anything or tell anyone because they won't believe you."

He raped me that night and again the following night. I couldn't comprehend why the man I loved and looked up to so much would do such a thing. I felt helpless; unable to defend myself. My screams dissolved into the dark shadows of my bedroom. My body turned lifeless and limp like discarded trash at the side of the curb. I felt worthless, lonely, and afraid. When he rose from my bedside, I thought to myself, "I could never share this horrific experience with anyone." He took the most precious thing in life from me, my virginity. A few days later, he put me on a plane and sent me home to Detroit.

I never told my mom what happened or why I never spoke of this despicable, evil man again for decades. I bottled up this incident, carefully tucking it deep down in my memory. Only, at the time, I didn't know or understand how it would resurface in the near future.

Rejection From My Biological Father

Upon graduating from Henry Ford High School, I knew I wanted to go to the University of Detroit. I had no desire to work for the Big Three auto companies–General Motors, Chrysler, or Ford. Detroit, known as the Motor City, considered it prestigious to work for one of them. The mentality was to graduate from high school and get a job working on the assembly line, but I wanted more than that. It was the only college I applied to and I was accepted into the Computer Science program. After just one semester, I was informed that I wouldn't be able to afford tuition without financial assistance. I didn't know anything about financial aid or loans. The financial aid office shared that I could use my father's Veterans' Assistance to reduce the tuition cost. As a single parent of three daughters, my mom couldn't afford college tuition. One afternoon, I swallowed my pride and walked to a phone booth outside of White Castle on Grand River and Southfield Freeway to call him. Why a phone booth? I didn't want anyone to hear me ask him for anything. There goes that pride again.

My father is a Vietnam veteran, and I could have used his military benefits to offset my tuition. The only reason I reached out was because I wanted to attend college. I had not spoken to him since the rape, now I needed him to provide his military information to the university.

It was December and the cold, icy, arctic air felt almost unbearable as I walked to the phone booth. With each step, I replayed the rape in my mind, trying to convince myself that he might feel remorseful for what he did to me and want to help me go to college. My nerves were on edge as I dialed his number. I kept thinking, *How will you react when you hear his voice?*

After three rings, he answered. My heart stopped for a moment. I tried to speak immediately following his, "Hello," but the words were caught in my throat. I nervously identified myself, and before he could interrupt me, I explained the reason for my call.

"Daddy, I'm attending the University of Detroit studying computer science but I can't afford the tuition any longer. I need your help. Can you please call the financial aid office and give them your veterans information so I can get a reduced tuition?"

He replied quickly, "No–it would be a waste of my money because you're a girl and you're just going to get married and have kids. Now if you were your brother, Donald, I would help you because he's a boy." Donald was my half brother, and one of about eight half siblings that he fathered over the years.

His response was so demoralizing, demeaning, and devaluing of my self-worth. It was a vicious and disheartening attack that I didn't think I could bounce back from. I hung up the phone and sobbed uncontrollably the entire way home. The freezing wind quickly dried my tears, and by the time I stepped through my front doors, I'd decided to join the United States Air Force. My father's side of the family were proud military folks from every branch of the service. Most of the men were lifers, meaning they retired from the military. I knew the Air Force was where I needed to be as they placed a significant emphasis on education. All I wanted to do was go to college and I enlisted a few weeks later. I served a total of six years in the military.

You might be wondering how I could praise God after everything that happened in my first 18 years of life. I'm a survivor, and that's exactly why I can give God praise. My experiences empower me to help others who have endured incest rape.

Heart Check-In

There's a fine line between love and hate. When something tragic happens in our lives, it cuts so deeply that we struggle to comprehend the pain. It's a pain unlike anything we've ever experienced or imagined—a whirlwind of indescribable emotions. How do we process such hurt from someone we loved and believed loved us in return?

> The aftermath leaves us withdrawn, suspicious, untrusting, and afraid to love again. The love we once freely gave transforms into a deeply hidden hatred. Thoughts of vengeance, haunting nightmares, and overwhelming emotions begin to overshadow our happiness. In these moments, we may wonder: How can we find even a glimpse of joy? All we want is to smile again, to feel a spark of happiness in our lives.
>
> There is hope. That glimmer of light begins to shine when we shift our focus toward positivity. Surrounding ourselves with positive influences can feel almost impossible at first, but we must be determined. We cannot let this person's wicked actions steal any more of our lives. It's time to reclaim our power and take control.
>
> I know you can do it because I did. It starts with a decision—a decision to move forward and a commitment to exercise that choice every single day. I won't sugarcoat it; the journey will be tough and at times, it will feel like too much to bear. But you cannot give up! You are God's child, a winner, and you will overcome. Keep going, and victory will be yours.

The military experience was far from pleasant. During basic training, we faced a simulated gas chamber drill that has caused lasting trauma for veterans to this day. This difficult environment was compounded by my military tour, where I experienced racism for the first time in my life. There were numerous painful incidents where I was subjected to racist slurs but felt unable to respond or express my emotions. The military was my lifeline to education, and showing any emotion could mean failing basic training and being sent home.

Arriving in Rapid City, South Dakota, I immediately felt a sense of uncertainty. The bus ride to Ellsworth Air Force Base (AFB) was unlike anything I had experienced before, especially for a young Black woman who had never traveled to the Midwest. Looking around the bus, I didn't see anyone who resembled me, all while trying to erase the unsettling memories of the last few weeks of basic training. My only frame of reference had been the stories my grandparents shared when I visited them in the South, and the images I'd seen in movies. When we arrived at Ellsworth AFB, we were placed in a room where we were sternly warned to avoid certain areas. They told us that by the time the Air Force reached you, it might be too late.

I remember a trip to the mall where little children pointed and hid behind their mother's leg, having never seen a Black person before. The reality hit me hard when I was leaving, and heard three men pointing at us, saying, "Look at the n****r with the box." It was demeaning, yet we had to contain ourselves and walk slowly, making no sudden movements as we made our way to the car to leave.

In recent years, it had been revealed that Ellsworth AFB was contaminated with asbestos for decades, resulting in long-term health issues for many military personnel, some of whom are still suffering from its effects today. During my time in the military, I was not able to complete a degree. Although local colleges offered weekly courses on base, the credits I earned weren't enough to fulfill the requirements of a full degree.

How can I still praise God after going through that hell? At that point in my life, I hadn't given my heart to Christ, but He was quietly building my inner strength–strength I wouldn't truly recognize until years later.

During that ordeal, I felt a fierce determination to succeed and pursue a college education, no matter the challenges I faced. Looking back on those days, I smile thinking of how I persevered, and how I said my prayers every night.

I also met two of my sister-friends, Jan and Mae. They've been closer than family, offering support and love since I was 18. I consider this friendship a true blessing, as we've always been there for each other.

Over the years, I earned three degrees and several certifications: an Associate of Applied Science in Electrical Engineering Technology, a Bachelor of Science in Business Management and Information Systems, and a Master of Science in Computer Information Systems. God had blessed me with the desires of my heart. When I pursued my associate degree, I took out student loans, using the refunds to cover rent, food, and other expenses for myself and my son, Paul. I also worked part-time. After graduating, I faced the task of repaying those loans, so I deferred as much as I could.

How can I praise God for my student loan debt? I'm glad you asked. Even though I hadn't given my life to Christ at that time, He still blessed me. The loans provided the means to give my son shelter, food, and daycare without the need for public assistance. Were there times when things felt extremely tight and stressful? Absolutely. Financial support didn't always come in the way I had hoped, but God always provided.

There were times when there was only enough food for Paul, so I would go without eating for a couple of days, waiting for my paycheck from my part-time job. He never knew there wasn't enough for both of us because I'd simply say, "I'm not hungry." Through it all, we must remember that God is our provider, and He is always faithful to His word. It's important to pause and reflect on gratitude. Despite the challenges, we had a warm apartment, clean clothes, and enough gas in the car to get us to work and school. I like to remind myself to take a moment to give thanks for the blessings I have no matter how difficult my journey might seem.

Let's pause for a moment...Name one thing that you're grateful for today.

A couple of years later, when I surrendered my life to God, something incredible happened with those student loans. I received promissory notes in the mail, each one stamped "Paid in Full." I couldn't believe it, so I called the company to confirm and they verified that my loans were paid off. Tears flowed like a river.

When I later pursued my BS and MS, I worked for DirecTV and they paid my full tuition, including books. No student loan debt.

Blessings don't always come in the way we expect; we have to embrace the ups and downs and keep looking up. Look at my younger self who was raped by her father, who later refused to assist with my college tuition because I wasn't a man. I'm incredibly grateful that God created me with inner strength, determination, and the drive to stand tall, hold my head high, push my shoulders back, and face adversity, pain, disappointment, and life's challenges with confidence and faith, knowing God is always with me.

If He did it for me, know that He will do it for you, too. I know it might seem difficult to let your guards down and trust anyone. God isn't anyone, He's the one above us all. Take a leap of faith and give God an opportunity to love you. You have nothing to lose, and everything to gain.

True Forgiveness: Do I Want to Forgive? How Can I Forgive?

On October 2nd, 1993, during a revival in Cherry Hill, New Jersey, I said, "Yes," to the Lord, and my life was changed forever. When I returned to my home on October 3rd I was still on a spiritual high from the night before. I started pulling my micro-mini skirts out of the closet, packing them up to donate to Goodwill. As someone who thrives on organization, I began restructuring my daily routines to include a dedicated time for reading and meditation on the Word. Each morning at 6 a.m., I would curl up in my favorite oversized chair, ready to start the day in reflection.

One morning during my prayer time, the Lord instructed me to write a letter to my biological father, telling him that I forgave him. Oh my goodness, I didn't see that coming. Prayer ended abruptly that morning. I found myself at a loss for words, unsure of how I felt. Emotions I thought were buried suddenly surged to the surface, overwhelming me. I curled up in that chair, feeling like a fetus in the womb, I'm still unsure of how long I sat there.

I kept questioning whether I truly wanted to forgive him. I envisioned him on the ground, begging for my help as he was dying, and I knelt down and whispered in his ear, "You're already dead to me," before getting up and walking away without looking back. I had no idea I had feelings like that buried deep inside. It didn't feel Christian at all, and I struggled with that too. I couldn't process why God would ask me to write a letter to tell this man that I had forgiven him for raping me.

I remember crying until I made myself sick. I kept asking God, "Why? Why would you have me do that? Why?" One morning while reading my Bible, I was led to 1 Samuel 15:22 (NKJV) which said, "Behold, to obey is better than sacrifice." The crying frenzy started all over again. I was torn between being obedient to what the Lord instructed me to do and being defiant and stubborn. I felt like he was getting a *get out of jail free* card by forgiving him. Part of me wanted him to feel the pain I felt that I had buried for years. After a couple of weeks, I decided to adhere to God's guidance. Why? Because I loved God more than life and if He asked me to write this letter, I would obey. That was the beginning of me humbling my strong and stubborn will to do things my way.

Once I started writing the letter a flood of emotions began rising up again. My thoughts went dark. The thought of him reading the letter and mocking me crossed my mind, along with how he violated me without consequences. I persevered by praying and asking God to take away those thoughts with every word I wrote. The letter simply said,

I gave my life to Christ and He told me to write this letter to you. I forgive you because I must forgive you. The Bible says, "Beloved, let us love one

another, for love is of God; and everyone who loves is born of God and knows God" (1 John 4:7 NKJV). You will have to stand before God and account for your sins, I don't have a heaven or hell to put you in, therefore I forgive you for raping me, but I don't want a relationship with you.

I sealed the envelope, but I was still having mixed feelings. I wondered why. I was being obedient by writing the letter. My mind kept telling me to rip the letter up and throw it in the trash. It bothered me to the point that I actually got in my jeep and drove to a mailbox, dropped it in, and drove away. The moment the mailbox door closed, I felt an overwhelming sense of freedom, like a bird that could once only fly a few feet off the ground but was now soaring high in the sky, smiling and singing.

I thought it was over, and that I was free. Unfortunately, that feeling was short-lived. A few days later, I received a phone call. Guess who was on the other end? Yes, it was him. The voice said, "Hey, this is your daddy, and I received your letter." It was as if my wings were clipped, and I was falling out of the sky and the ground was approaching quickly. I couldn't speak for a moment. He kept saying it was good to receive a letter from me. Finally, I repeated what I wrote in the letter, hoping he would hang up. But he didn't. I was so caught off guard that I couldn't even pray, I was stuck like a deer caught in headlights. It was as if my whole world stopped, and I was caught in the twilight zone.

He said, "I would like to come see you and the kid." The kid was my son, Paul. How did he know so much about me and my life? He must have been communicating with my mother and sisters. Something snapped inside of me when he mentioned the kid. I said, "I don't want a relationship with you, and I don't want you near my son. I was being obedient to the Lord, so please don't call me again." I couldn't understand why God would allow him to call me; I'd written the letter and forgiven him. I couldn't pray or even ask why for a few hours. I finally asked God, "Why did You allow him to call me? I did what you told me to do, I wrote the letter, why God? Why?" The only comforting word that I received from the Lord was "I'm proud of you." As I grew in the Word and after years, I finally understood that the forgiveness was not for him, but for me. Mark 11:25 NKJV says, "And whenever you stand praying, if you have anything against anyone, forgive him, that your Father in heaven may also forgive you your trespasses."

Heart Check-In

Forgiveness may seem impossible at first - how could we possibly forgive after such pain? But then comes a moment of clarity: by holding onto our anger, we're letting them continue to control us. We become prisoners of our own grudges, our emotions pulled like strings by someone who likely doesn't even think about what they did. While they move freely through life, we remain stuck, trapped by our own resentment. We deserve more than this. We deserve to embrace life fully, to cherish time with family, and to create beautiful new memories. It's time to break free and truly live - because that's what we deserve.

Rejection From My Sibling

A few years ago, I helped my first cousin, Lynn with one of her events, and we took photos that we later posted on Facebook. A few days later, we discovered our photo appeared on an adult sex site linked to my biological father. I was furious and my cousin was upset as well. In response, I posted a private message only him, my sisters, some of my cousins, uncles and aunts on his side of the family would be able to see. In this private post, I shared that he raped me when I was 14 years old and if he didn't take that post down, I would expose him to all of the family. I told him to never, ever, ever, attempt to contact me or my children. My baby sister was so enraged that she stopped speaking to me. She wasn't angry at what he did to me, she was outraged that I shared it with his family.

My middle sister, Tonya, was very supportive. I received love and support from my first cousins in his family which I was grateful for. You're probably wondering if I ever shared my tragic past with my children and the answer is: yes. I told Paul when he was 16 years old, and I'll delve into that later. I didn't share it with my daughter, Monica until she was 13 years old, but when I did, it helped her understand why I'd been overprotective.

Forty-six years later in 2023, I saw my biological father at a family gathering. I avoided him. This was noticeable to the family, so he came and stood next to me during the family photo. Of course, I moved to the other side of one of my uncles. He immediately walked up to me after the photo. I couldn't avoid him quickly enough, so I had to stand there and listen to him. He said, "Can I talk to you before you leave?" He avoided making eye-contact. Those buried feelings rose again. I wanted to jump up, do a roundhouse, and drop kick him. I went into the bathroom and prayed. I thought I had forgiven him, and that I was free. But in that moment, I understood why the Lord led me to fast for three days before the family gathering.

As I prepared to leave, he wanted to talk to me, but not in private. He wanted to talk outside in the parking lot where the rest of the family were chatting. He strategically positioned himself with his back toward them and I was facing them.

He started by saying, "I was on drugs and I was messed up." But when I looked into his eyes, I saw no remorse, only evil. I could tell he hadn't changed, and I knew he didn't mean anything he was saying. After a couple of minutes, I'd had enough of the foolishness. I told him:

> I understand now why God had me fast for three days before coming here. He knew you would be here. You don't mean anything you're saying–you're just trying to save face with the family. I waited 46 years for you to acknowledge what you did, but I'm good. You're still the same person. At least I had the chance to look you in the eye, tell you I'm okay, and that God has blessed me.

Heart Check-In

Have you ever thought you had forgiven someone, only to see them years later and find those old feelings of hurt resurfacing, leaving you confused?

I found out for 46 years I had been grieving from the rape. I forgave him like the Lord instructed me to do. But I had buried those emotions so deep that I didn't feel it any longer. I buried them so deep that I forgot about them. When I buried them, I assumed they would never rise again, that they were dead. That wasn't the reality of my forgiveness. Just like a death I had to grieve. The grieving was over when I was able to hear him acknowledge what he did to me.

Take a moment and think about something that you have suppressed. Allow yourself to grieve so you can heal. Don't rush the process, take your time so that you're completely free.

Do you want to know what this man had the audacity to say next? Wait for it. He asked, "Can I call you sometime?" I started walking away. But then, with some family close by, he says, "Let's take a picture." I was speechless as he handed his phone to one of my cousins. It was the Holy Spirit that glued my mouth shut. I couldn't say a word. I was beyond outdone.

God, why? Why is this man doing this? Why are you allowing him to do this? As quickly as those questions were coming to mind, I felt the embrace of the Holy Spirit. I felt His presence, calming me, reminding me that everything was okay and that He was with me. As I stood there, waiting for them to take that picture, I knew that God had me in His arms.

God is so good. My second cousin, Karen, came and stood next to me before they took the picture. I thanked her quietly. She was my support and little did she know how much her hug and intervention meant to me.

God is a provider. Following that photo, I got in my car and drove home. I finally understood the act of forgiveness and closure. I thought I had forgiven him. I guess I had in words, but not in my heart. When I drove away, I could truly say I'd forgiven him and that I was free. It's hard to describe the new freedom I'd found. Now, I understand a bit more about why it took me 46 years. I went through many stages of unforgiveness, thinking that I had graduated to forgiveness, but I was mistaken. I hadn't acknowledged the grieving that goes with forgiveness.

I believe that forgiveness is a journey that often mirrors the five stages of grief: denial, anger, bargaining, depression, and acceptance. During this spiritual journey, we might not even realize we're grieving. We're often taught that simply saying "I forgive you" should instantly erase the pain, betrayal, and abuse. But that's not always true.

Forgiveness often begins with denial, which can manifest as vivid nightmares or a desperate hope that we'll wake up and find it was all just a bad dream. But reality doesn't change, and those hidden feelings of hurt begin to surface as anger. Sometimes, we unknowingly take that anger out on others—acting bitter, short-tempered, or resentful. Have you ever experienced denial and anger after trying to forgive someone? I have, and it's okay. It's part of the process. Acknowledging these emotions means you're on your way to complete forgiveness.

Next comes bargaining, where the "what-ifs" start to overwhelm us. We replay painful memories, wondering if things could have been different. "What if I had done this? Maybe the outcome would have changed." These thoughts often turn into misplaced blame, convincing us that it was our fault. But let me be clear: it wasn't your fault. The responsibility lies solely with the person who caused the harm. Remember, you're a survivor, and that alone speaks volumes about your strength and resilience.

As you near the finish line of forgiveness, depression might try to pull you back. It creeps in quietly, bringing feelings of isolation, sleeplessness, and difficulty concentrating. When this happens, don't hesitate to seek professional help. Finding a therapist or emotional support is not a sign of weakness; it's an essential step to overcoming depression and reclaiming your peace.

Finally, acceptance arrives. Acceptance doesn't mean forgetting or moving past the grief entirely. It means understanding how the experience shaped your life and deciding how to move forward. After 46 years of my own grieving process, I've found that acceptance also brings purpose. I now see how God transformed my pain—an incest rape—into an opportunity to minister to others and show how He turns sorrow into joy.

Take the time to grieve. Allow yourself to feel every emotion, and trust that once the process is complete, you'll walk in the fullness of forgiveness. It's not easy, but it's worth it.

This forgiveness journey is part of my ministry, and I believe God took me through this valley so I could be a vessel to minister to His people in the days to come.

I believe that one day my siblings will come to understand my spiritual journey. This path wasn't one I chose; it's the one God created me for, so that I could serve as a vessel to help His people. I pray for them, trusting that in time, their journeys would become testimonies that bring God glory.

CHAPTER 2

It's Okay To Start Over At Any Age And Stage Of Your Life

---※---

Friends Were My Village Not Family

Throughout this journey I've been blessed with a phenomenal circle of friends who were and are my rocks, my trusted confidants, my prayer warriors, and my extended family who have walked with me, cried with me, and supported me every step of the way. The village began to take shape in 1982 during my military career at Ellsworth Air Force Base, South Dakota where I met Jan and Mae.

Jan and I shared a dormitory room while Mae lived just down the hall. From the moment we met, the bond was instantaneous, as if we'd known each other forever. Jan was my third roommate, and we quickly discovered how much we had in common–down to our shared obsession with cleanliness. Our beds were made every morning, clothes were always put away, and dirty dishes were never left in the sink. Most importantly, our shared bathroom was always spotless and smelling good.

Though Jan and I both grew up in Detroit, Michigan, we never crossed paths until we became roommates. Mae, on the other hand, was originally from Las Vegas, Nevada. With her natural charm and warmth, she drew people in, and her presence made any room feel brighter.

TEARS OF FAITH

The three of us each had different roles in the military: Jan managed classified documents, Mae interacted with security, and I was a systems analyst. On our base, there were only 33 African-American women, and we lived in a coed barrack–females on the first floor and males on the second.

As city girls, we had to navigate the elements to get to work by 7 a.m. using a personal vehicle. Before it was called carpooling, we were already sharing rides with others from the dorms who owned vehicles. I vaguely remember a government van offering rides, but I also recall trudging through snow that could reach 30-40 inches with wind chills below 30 degrees.

Dressed in our long green insulated parkas, designed to keep us warm and dry, along with matching mukluk boots and gloves, we braved the harsh cold. The base commander even issued warnings to airmen, advising them to avoid snow ditches, as falling in could leave you completely unfindable until the snow melted.

Mae was also a talented DJ at the airman's club and off-base, captivating everyone with her sensual radio voice. Her musical performances usually took place on Wednesday and Saturday nights, with occasional gigs on Sundays and Mondays, depending on the holidays. On those nights, Jan and I were always there to support her, dancing the night away. We'd arrive before the club opened and stay long after it closed, always with big smiles on our faces, yet we never missed work at 7 a.m. the next day.

After about a year in the dorms, the three of us moved into apartments in the same complex. From our windows, we could see each other's buildings–close enough to feel connected, but with enough space to maintain our independence. We valued our privacy and always respected each other's space, never dropping by unannounced.

Jan was the first to leave the pack as her tour ended, followed by me. Mae actually made a career out of the Air Force and retired after more than 20 years. Over the years we kept in touch. My children refer to Jan as "Aunt Jan," and while they've never met Mae, they've heard countless stories about her. Jan has been with me through the ups and downs of my life. I've shared intimate secrets with her and she has never betrayed my trust. Our motto is simple: "This is a safe space." It's our way of saying, "I'm here to help you, to support you, and to be open and honest in our discussions."

In 1987, my village grew with the addition of Dee Dee, followed by Camille in 1997, and Carlie in 2002. In 1987, while in Rochester, NY I started visiting Celeste Salon, where Dee Dee's mother did my hair. Dee Dee herself, was a highly sought-after stylist, professional model, and the wife of a pastor. This was during my partying phase, yet despite that, she and I became friends. She never judged me for being a clubber, and I often remind her that her kindness and non-judgemental nature contributed to my walk with Christ. Afterall, she witnessed my transformation from sinner to Christian.

> **Heart Check-In**
>
> "For by grace you have been saved through faith, and that not of yourselves; it is the gift of God, not of works, lest anyone should boast." (Ephesians 2:8-9)
>
> God forgives us and washes away our sins because He loves us. When we surrender to God and decide to live a Christian life, it doesn't mean we're perfect or immune to making mistakes–because we will. Being a Christian doesn't make us better than anyone else. It simply means that God's grace has given us the desire to worship and follow Him by faith, trusting in His presence every step of the way, even when we can't see the future.

> Never let anyone, Christian or non-Christian, make you feel bad or doubt yourself for not having given your life to Christ yet. Everyone has their own moment, their own "timestamp," for when they will choose to surrender to God.
>
> God loved me and protected me when I was in the clubs, partying. He never turned His back on me, and He never will. Always remember: God loves you unconditionally, and nothing you do can change that.

I eventually became a member of Newborn Fellowship Christian Center where Dee Dee and Bishop, her husband, served as pastors. During that time, I confided in her my deepest, undisclosed, and innermost secrets—stories of a failed marriage, personal hurts, challenges in my faith walk, and countless tears. She listened, encouraged, and prayed for me.

In 1997, my sister circle expanded with Camille. We met when I moved to California to marry Sam, my ex, and she even attended my wedding. From the start, we shared an instant connection and over the years it has become an impenetrable bond. We attended Center of Christ Ministries together until I relocated to North Carolina. Over the years, we have taken "girl trips" to ensure we're making time for ourselves.

Camille is humble, meek, and reserved but don't be fooled—she is a powerful prayer warrior. Whenever I need an intercessor to pray with me and for me, she's the one I turn to. Like I've shared previously, what is said in my village of sisterhood, stays within the village. It's a safe place, and I'm grateful for the unwavering, accepting, protective, and loving support we share.

In 2002, Carlie became a part of my inner sisterhood circle. Paul was a junior in high school at the time, and that was the first year he attended a public school. Our sons played football together, became best friends, and still are. I met Carlie at one of their football games. We sat next to each other on the bleachers and chatted about how cold it was outside. It was an instant connection.

I began visiting her church and women's events and she did the same for me. We quickly discovered that we both shared a love for fashion. Carlie loves the Lord and has a sweet, gentle spirit of servitude and excellence. Whenever I need a listening ear or a sounding board, I call Carlie. She graciously offers thoughtful feedback, in alignment with the Bible. Then, hold on, she's going to break it down in a raw, unfiltered, everyday version too.

All of these amazing women have been by my side as I navigated my journey–from discovering my identity as a young lady, embracing my youth and singleness to dating, marriage, childbirth, divorce, and the growth that came with tears of faith.

My circle of sisterhood spans many decades, and I'm grateful for the blessing of having them walk with me through it all. They've encouraged me, held me up when I was too weak to stand, cried with me and wiped my tears, answered my calls in the middle of the night, and stayed on the phone until the sun came up. They've celebrated my successes, laughed with me, and provided honest, constructive feedback–even when I didn't want to hear it.

Our value system is simple: a safe place. This kind of environment—where trust and confidentiality are core values—fosters deeper, more meaningful discussions. When everyone feels safe to share openly, it builds strong bonds and creates a supportive space where all thoughts and feelings are respected and protected. The assurance of privacy is incredibly empowering.

When evaluating friendships, choose people who have kind, caring hearts, and share core values like integrity, selflessness, positivity, encouragement, trust, and a willingness to listen. Along the way, you might encounter individuals with toxic tendencies. These are relationships that will not be beneficial to you. Relationships that lack safety, trust, and mutual encouragement can drain your energy and leave you feeling unseen. If someone isn't willing or able to reciprocate genuine care, it's a clear sign to protect your emotional well-being.

The phrase, "Stop, drop, and roll," is a perfect analogy here—it's about saving yourself from the emotional fire before it causes lasting harm. Choosing friends who mirror your kindness and values, ensures that your energy is invested in connections that uplift and support you.

Repairing a Broken Heart

The courtship started in 1995 with a blind date.

Sam was the best man at the wedding of our mutual friend, Terry. It took some convincing from Terry for me to even consider a blind date. I repeatedly told him I didn't want to meet anyone, especially an evangelist. After days of coaxing, I finally agreed. The plan was for us to meet during the wedding reception, and go on our first date to the movies the next day. Unfortunately, he missed his flight and couldn't attend the wedding or the reception. Upon arriving in Rochester, New York, he got my phone number from Terry and called to ask if he could stop by my home to introduce himself.

The phone call was brief, and I got straight to the point in a sweet, kind, and gentle voice, "No, you cannot stop by my home. I don't know you, and it's inappropriate. It's too late—my son is in bed sleeping. I don't expose my son to men unless I know their character and have determined what role, if any, they will play in my life."

The next day, before going to the movies, we met at Terry's parents' home, who were pastors. I picked him up in my blue 1995 Isuzu Rodeo. It was our first date and I wore a beige sleeveless, button-down maxi sundress, gold accessories, gold strappy sandals, and a small gold handbag. The bottom three buttons of my dress were unbuttoned. When Pastor Celeste noticed, with a smile, she whispered in my ear, "Button it up."

At the concession stand, Sam raided the place, purchasing popcorn, Twizzlers, a hotdog, and a soda. I didn't get anything to eat but when he offered to share his popcorn, I had a little. He was a perfect gentleman.

After the movie, we returned to the pastor's house so Sam could confirm his next preaching engagement. He apologized for making the phone calls during our time together. My response was simple, "Handle your business, so when you're finished, it'll be my time." The look on his face was priceless. He laughed and said in his commanding, deep voice, "No woman has ever said that to me."

I smiled and replied, "I guess you haven't really encountered someone like me before."

He chuckled, and we both burst out laughing. In the COGIC (Church of God In Christ) world, he was considered someone of great stature. Over the next couple days, we spent time together–movies, dinner, and laughing uncontrollably. It was refreshing. I had chosen not to date after giving my life to Christ in 1993. My focus was on developing my relationship with Christ and raising Paul.

Sam shared a bit about his family dynamics, mentioning that he had six siblings. They were all really close, which I thought was nice.

On Tuesday afternoon, I drove him to the airport so he could catch his flight back home to California. While we were there, he asked if I'd be interested in flying to California to meet his family. I hesitated, as we'd only known each other for two days, but he reassured me, saying his family would love to meet me, and even offered for me to stay at his sister's place. I accepted his invitation and after leaving the airport, I immediately called Dee Dee to discuss the offer and to get her opinion. She and her family had known Sam for decades and were familiar with his character, so I valued her insight as she was part of my sister circle.

When he suggested I stay at his sister's home, I realized he was referencing Romans 14:16, which speaks about not letting our good be spoken of as evil and acting with kindness and hospitality. Essentially, if I stayed at a hotel, he wouldn't be able to pick me up because it could be perceived as inappropriate. I was perfectly comfortable with the arrangement to stay at his sister's residence.

He flew back to California, and the next day, he called to get the details of my visit. Shortly after, he sent me a roundtrip, first-class ticket.

Heart Check-In

"Therefore do not let your good be spoken of as evil." (Romans 14:16)

There are times when you have good intentions but they're misperceived as evil. If I stayed in a hotel and someone saw Sam picking me up, the assumption would have been that we spent the night together. That untrue assumption could possibly hinder a person's walk with Christ. It could also damage his ministry as one could assume that a man of God wasn't living what he was preaching.

> Have you ever had someone jump to the wrong conclusion and start spreading evil rumors, not knowing the facts? Just think about the fallout that would have on your emotions, your career, your family. That's what the fallout would have been if I stayed at a hotel without a chaperone. The perception alone could have caused harm, both to my integrity and to the integrity of the ministry.

On February 21st, 1995, I arrived in Los Angeles, California and he was late picking me up. Yep, you see the pattern—I'm a stickler for being on time, so needless to say, I had a serious attitude. He finally arrived about 30 minutes late, carrying roses and an apology. It took me a while to shake off my attitude. I had to talk myself into letting it go, especially since I'd flown all the way across the country and was only going to be there for a couple of days.

I had dressed cute for the occasion—a chocolate brown sweater and a cream leather skirt that hit just above the knee, complemented by cream leather pumps. Little did I know, our date would begin at Universal Citywalk in Hollywood and I was wearing 3-inch heels. Like a true diva, I remained in character. I walked around in those heels for about five hours. Afterward, we drove about 90 minutes to his sister's home in San Bernardino, where I spent the night and was promptly interrogated.

The interrogation questions:
- When did you meet Sam?
- How did you meet?
- How old is your son?
- What's your son's name?
- Has he met Sam yet?
- Where do you work?

- Do you own your own home?
- Do you have a college education?
- If so, what's your degree?

I smiled and provided simple responses as to not be disrespectful, also saying don't cross the line with your questioning. Through the interrogation, she let it slip that I was the first woman Sam had brought home to meet his family.

The next morning, he was there bright and early to pick me up, eager to introduce me to his mother and some of his friends. Later, we met the rest of his family for dinner at a restaurant along the Pacific Coast Highway. I answered their questions about my education, being a single mother, working, and affording private school for Paul with grace and confidence, reflecting the strength and determination that defined who I was. That night, I stayed at his mother's home.

The next morning, he picked me up early, and we had breakfast before he drove me to the airport on February 23rd. On the way to Los Angeles International Airport, he started reciting poetry by Langston Hughes. I'm not sure how he knew I loved poetry, but it struck a positive chord with me. At that moment, I thought to myself, "Alright, I'm open and ready to embrace whatever comes next." As we sat at the gate, and waited for me to board the flight back home, he asked if we could date exclusively. I smiled and replied, "Yes." He embraced me with a loving hug and kissed me on the cheek.

For this to be a long-distance relationship, he truly swept me off my feet. The longest we ever went without seeing each other was about 4-5 weeks but we spoke on the phone almost every night. The first time I received a phone bill of $900, I just about went into cardiac arrest. Sam paid every phone bill without a second thought. He would bring me roses, and there would always be a gift inside–money, jewelry, or handwritten poems that he would later recite to me. Yep, I was smitten.

He respected my boundaries and privacy, which was important to me. After a few months, he asked when I was going to introduce him to Paul. He was charming and captivating, but I wasn't sure if I was ready for that step just yet. I politely replied, "I'm not sure where we stand yet or where this relationship is going, so I can't entertain introductions at this time."

> ### Heart Check-In
>
> "Keep your heart with all diligence, For out of it spring the issues of life." (Proverbs 4:23)
>
> Protect your heart because heartache creates obstacles in life.
>
> As a single parent, I was cautious about introducing people to my son unless I was sure they would have a positive and lasting impact. When dating, I always thought about the potential aftermath if the relationship didn't work out. What if my son became attached, and the breakup affected him? How would it impact his heart, and how long might it take for him to heal? Is dating this person worth exposing his heart?
>
> Being a single parent involves many sacrifices as we nurture our children to adulthood. It's acceptable to voice and stand on your standards, expectations, and protection of any child's heart.

He understood and respected how protective I was as a mother. The rule was simple: if he called and Paul answered, his only response could be, "May I please speak to Sheila?" If my son asked who was calling or if I wasn't available, he could not leave his name; instead, he would say, "OK, I will call back." He honored my decision, and after almost a year of dating, I formally introduced him to Paul.

We dated for two years and only a handful of people knew about our relationship. I wasn't a church groupie who hung around after the services to flirt with the evangelists. In fact, unless he was preaching at my church, I didn't go hear him minister. I flew back to California to celebrate our two-year anniversary. Inevitably, I forgot his mother's birthday was on the same day, and I was heartbroken that we didn't have a special dinner to commemorate our day. His family took his mother to dinner to celebrate her birthday which was wonderful and made her happy, but everyone could see the disappointment in my eyes. I didn't receive roses or even a poem that night.

The restaurant was right on the beach. Following dinner, I decided to take a stroll alone, along the shore in my suede booties–a decision that only highlighted my disappointment. Suede and sand, as it turns out, are not a winning combination.

He later came to talk to me. I was so upset I couldn't find any words. I remained silent. Afterward, he took me to his mother's house for the night. The next morning, bright and early, he wanted to take me for a ride in the mountains. But I was still holding onto my attitude and wasn't in the mood to go. My flight was leaving the next day, and all I really wanted was to go home. After several apologies, I finally agreed to go for the ride.

All the way up the mountain, he kept playing a song by Bill Withers–*Just the Two of Us*. When we arrived near a lake on the mountainside, he suggested we have a picnic. I declined as it was freezing outside. Finally, he threw the blanket on the armrest between the two front seats and started singing the song he had been playing for the last half hour.

Then he pushed his seat all the way back and tried to maneuver his body to face me completely. At 6'2" and about 220 pounds, it was a humorous sight to me. We both glared at each other for a moment before bursting into uncontrollable laughter. Finally, he settled into a position, gazed into my eyes, and proposed to me. In response, I gave him a heartfelt kiss.

"You didn't answer, will you marry me?" he asked.

I smiled and replied with an affirmative, "Yes." As we drove down the mountain, the first person we called was Paul, who stayed with a close friend while I was in California. He was so excited, and asked, "When you and Mommy get married, can I call you Daddy?" Sam's face lit up like a Christmas tree, and he said, "Yes."

Five months later, we were married.

May 28th, Paul and I packed the U-haul, drove my Rodeo onto an auto transport, hitched it to the back of the U-Haul in preparation for our cross country relocation to California. Sam was scheduled to fly in from his preaching engagement on May 28th. The three of us would experience the cross-county adventure together in anticipation of becoming a family. His engagement was extended for 3 days. My lease ended on May 29th and I did not want to try and secure temporary housing so I made the decision for Paul and I to proceed with the cross-country move. Early May 29th, we climbed into the U-Haul with a map, snacks, his boombox, a mobile phone and started our road trip. Sam and Bishop objected to us driving across the country alone. They thought it wasn't safe for a woman and child. Maybe they were right, but I knew that God was with me and would watch over us.

We drove from 5:00 a.m. to 6:00 p.m. for 4 days, stopping for gas, food, and pre-selected hotels that could accommodate vehicles with trailers. Once Paul and I checked into the hotels we called Sam, Dee Dee and Bishop to let them know we arrived safely. We ate dinner at the hotel to reinforce safety. The road trip was a wonderful unforgettable memory for us. We had the opportunity to share a beautiful transition of being just the two of us to embarking on a new family dynamic. We arrived in California on June 1st. We never got lost or experienced any issues with the U-Haul. Praise God!

Bishop Charles E. Blake, Sr., of Los Angeles COGIC agreed to perform our wedding ceremony. First, we had to go through marriage counseling. Since I lived across the country in Rochester, NY, Bishop Blake arranged a two-day marriage counseling session in April. I flew to California for the sessions, but I had also scheduled a job interview with Microwave Communications, Inc. (MCI) on the first day. I was offered a position as the Field Engineer and I started work three weeks before our wedding date on July 12th. MCI allowed me to take a week off for our honeymoon.

I was so used to managing my own finances that the thought of depending on someone to take care of us was unimaginable. Subconsciously, I think I harbored the abuse my mother endured, and promised myself it would never happen to me. No man would ever have that type of control over me.

Throughout our courtship, we never delved deeply into discussions about marriage. Whenever he'd say, "One day," I'd quickly cut in and respond, "When you're sure, let me know. But I'm not the kind of woman who's going to wait around for years. My time is valuable, and I'm not waiting on anyone." He'd chuckle with that deep voice of his and reply, "I guess you told me," and we'd both laugh.

What we did discuss was my stance on not adopting all the church traditions imposed on women. I made it clear that if I married a man in the ministry, I was marrying *him*, not the church. He always liked that philosophy.

When you marry someone who preaches the Word of God, you step into a sacred partnership that requires divine anointing. As their spouse, you are called to be an intercessor, uplifter, and minister to your partner. Your role is to create a sanctuary at home where they can shed their ministerial duties and find rest in your love and understanding.

The minister's home should be a haven of peace, where they can transition from their public role to simply being themselves. Your love, kindness, and compassion should create a safe space where they can be vulnerable and renewed.

This calling requires a deep sense of self-worth and security. You must stand confident in your own position, free from jealousy or insecurity about your spouse's relationship with the congregation. Your heart should be expansive enough to pray sincerely for God's people, even when they challenge your patience.

Understanding your worth enables your spiritual gifts to flourish. When you walk in this confidence, you naturally display the leadership, power, and compassion that inspire others in their spiritual journey. These qualities become a source of encouragement for those watching your example.

I learned this truth firsthand. Though I would tell Sam, "The Lord didn't call me into ministry, and I didn't marry the church," I chose to embody the peace, love, and compassion that both my spouse and God's people needed. While maintaining my individual identity, I embraced the opportunity to support both my partner and the congregation through genuine care and understanding.

Our engagement was announced during a Sunday morning service and that's when the craziness from the Christian community began. I remember that after service, women would approach me, asking to see my engagement ring. When I'd show it to them, they'd often comment, "You're so lucky to be marrying him." He'd be within earshot, grinning like the Cheshire Cat. My response was always the same, "No, he's lucky to be marrying me. Look at me—I'm a rare jewel in his crown." And every time, he'd burst out laughing.

When the mothers of the church found out that my wedding dress was off-white, they held a meeting and decided I couldn't wear anything resembling white because I had a child. They insisted my dress needed to be a different color.

When I told the mothers to leave me alone, they turned to him, hoping he'd intervene. "What? Are you serious?" I asked him.

My words to him were:

> God gave me a vision of my dress long before I even met you. I saw that dress in a bridal magazine. When I went to the bridal shop to order it, I hadn't even met you yet, and the staff thought I was crazy for ordering a dress without a fiancé. In fact, the dress in the magazine had already been retired, they agreed to try and locate one that's similar. They told me not to get my hopes up. How did God bless me and confirm my vision? After a few weeks, I received a phone call from the bridal shop. They found the exact wedding dress in the magazine. It took me months to pay for my wedding dress which hung up in a closet months before I met you. Now, you or no one else is going to tell me that I can't wear it. You have a choice, either I'm wearing my dress, or we're not getting married.

He cracked-up and said, "All right then, I guess you told me." We both laughed.

Don't get me wrong—I'm pretty laid back, but I don't tolerate anyone criticizing my faith or meddling with my family. Our first real argument happened while we were planning the wedding, and it reached a point where people were even trying to decide what kind of wedding cake we should have. By the time we got to the rehearsal dinner, I whispered to him, "Let's just take Paul and go to Bishop Blake's office to get married." He stood up and put an end to all the chaos from family and friends. In the end, our wedding day was absolutely beautiful.

The marriage was great, until it wasn't. Out of respect for the ministry, for my ex, and for my children, I will not reveal the intimate details of what happened. I've never spoken disrespectfully about Sam to the children or to our families. *Why?* It was always my belief that what occurred between him and I was between the three of us—God, Sam, and me.

My children love their father, as they are meant to. They should never have to choose between us, and they shouldn't hear one parent speaking negatively about the other. They have the right to love both of us freely, and enjoy special moments with each parent, knowing that when they share those experiences, the other parent will be genuinely happy for them. They deserve the freedom to build positive relationships with both of us. Regardless of our disagreements, we remained cordial and respectful to one another.

What I will share, is my faith walk journey.

On Easter Sunday, March 31st, 2002, Sam was preparing to travel out of town. As was his usual routine, he would take our daughter to visit his mother before leaving. I saw this as the perfect opportunity for some much-needed alone time. I grabbed a piece of chicken, sat down in the family room, and turned on a television program of my choice. I can't recall where Paul, 16 years old, was at this time, but I was enjoying my "me, myself, and I" moment.

As I sat down to enjoy my chicken, I suddenly felt the presence of the Holy Spirit. I had to retreat to my bedroom, my prayer room, to pray. I'll never forget it. As I fell upon my knees to pray, the Lord spoke to me and said, "The walls around you are about to fall. Don't look to the left or to the right; keep your eyes on Me." I began to weep uncontrollably, and my mind immediately fell upon my children. Needless to say, I didn't eat that piece of chicken.

I don't remember how long I wept, but I wept until I was exhausted; I got into bed and went to sleep. I remember hearing Sam come home and put Monica to bed, and then tell me he was leaving for the airport. As usual, the alarm went off the next morning at 3:00 a.m. I got up with a heavy heart and prepared for my daily routine. I got ready for work, kissed Paul and told him to have a good day at school and that I would see him that evening. I grabbed Monica to drop her off at the in-home care provider by 4:30 a.m. and then started my one-hour commute to work.

However, this day felt different. My heart was heavy with the Word the Lord had given me the day before. I called Dee Dee, my trusted sister-friend in Rochester, NY. As I drove, I wept fiercely, telling her everything the Lord told me. All I could think about were my children–*was something going to happen to them?* She prayed with me and offered encouraging words, but still, that day felt unbearably long.

That night, I prayed earnestly. The next morning, during my commute, I called Sam to share the Word I had received. His response was simply, "Lord, Jesus."

By April 10th, 2002, the walls of my marriage came tumbling down. Despite the pain, God gave me the strength to hold my head high and follow His guidance. I couldn't understand why these things were happening. *I'm a good person*, I thought. *I worship You, Lord. I try to do the right thing.* Why was this happening? Did I do something wrong? If I did, I didn't realize it, and it was not intentional. Please forgive me.

My emotions swung from one extreme to the other, but I had to stay prayerful, or I feared I would have a nervous breakdown. I wanted my marriage to flourish, and failure wasn't an option. I didn't know what else to do but pray. I needed the inner strength only God could provide to help me get through my days at work and still be there for my children in the evenings.

After many weeks of questioning, the Lord spoke to me and said, "Fast and seek My face and I will move mountains out of your path." Four days later, the Lord woke me up by using Monica–*who slept in my bed like it was hers*– to kick her foot on the mattress in her sleep. I went downstairs and began to pray in my heavenly language. The Lord said, "My Hand is upon your children and no harm shall come near them. Fret not for I am with thee. For I have called thee. For you are chosen. For you will lay hands on My people. For you will prophesy to My daughters. I will restore everything that the cankerworm has eaten up."

The Lord knew how deeply I loved my children, and in that moment, He reassured me by waking me with a sense of peace. He reminded me that He was always there to protect them and walk beside me. He began to reveal glimpses of my purpose—why He created me and how I am meant to serve Him. He assured me not to worry, as He would restore everything I had lost.

The separation was inevitable. It happened and our home was on the market for sale shortly after. It sold quickly and I began my search for a house, options were scarce, and bidding wars were definite. I remember losing the bid on one house by $100 dollars. I was tired of searching for homes, putting in a bid only to find out I'd lost within a few hours. I just couldn't understand this valley that I was in, I knew that I had an intimate prayer life with God. The Lord continued to speak to me about various requests, but He never gave me an answer on why my marriage was falling apart.

During the trying time of our separation, even though my heart was shattered, I never said anything hurtful, degrading, or malicious towards him, to others, or to our daughter. As parents, we must remember that we are all God's children and no matter how I feel about a person, God still loves them. I always kept in mind that he was our daughter's father. I often reminded her, "That's your father, and you're supposed to love him." That still holds true today, and she's in her twenties.

> **Heart Check-In**
>
> "Death and life are in the power of the tongue." (Proverbs 18:21)
>
> It's crucial for parents to speak life and positivity into their children. I can only imagine how painful and confusing it must be for a child who feels pressured to choose between parents, fearing that loving one might hurt the other. Instead of freely enjoying the love of both parents, they may feel torn, caught in a competition they never asked to be part of, where each parent vies for their love and loyalty. The weight of trying to please both sides without appearing disloyal is an unfair burden for any child to carry. We should never let our children bear the cross of our anger, resentment, or unresolved hurt.
>
> Let's take a moment to pray that we never place the weight of choosing between parents on our children.

The Lord continued to speak to me, "I will give thee the desires of thy heart. I will restore everything. I will move mountains out of your path. I have called thee and you shall walk in the path that I have set for thee. For I AM with thee." At this point in the valley, I set aside the *why* and began to thank Him for loving me.

Sheila McDaniel

Emotionally Exhausted, Struggles of Single Parenting and Keeping the Faith

By October of 2002, the Lord blessed my children and I with a new home on Alabaster Court in Fontana, California. The Bible refers to alabaster as, "a woman [who] came to Him having an alabaster flask of very costly fragrant oil, and she poured it on His head as He sat at the table" (Matthew 26:7). This faith journey didn't promise an absence of challenges; in fact, there were many. But God was true, is true, and always will be true to His word.

All I knew was that the Lord had promised to take care of me, and if He said it, then it was so. The scripture says, *"If you have faith as a mustard seed, you will say to this mountain, 'Move from here to there,' and it will move; and nothing will be impossible for you,"* (Matthew 17:20). I've always had that kind of faith—the kind where, if the Lord said to speak to a mountain and it would move, I'd be the daughter who shows up every day with a tape measure, eager to see how far it had shifted.

The separation was incredibly challenging for us. Being a teenager, Paul struggled deeply, wrestling with anger and reexamining his faith. Being in California and far from family, I felt isolated, and my pride kept me from reaching out for help. I didn't want my children to see me break down or show any sign of weakness. What kind of example would that set for Paul, who had always seen me praying, fasting, and reassuring him that God would take care of us? I'll admit, some nights were overwhelming. After my children fell asleep, I'd slip into the furthest corner of my walk-in closet, pressing my hand over my mouth to stifle the sobs as I wept in silence. I called these, *"muffled cries"*—tears I shed in the quietest hours when words failed, and all I could do was cry. Though I couldn't find the strength to pray, I clung to the truth that God was faithful and wouldn't let me fall. As in Psalm 56:8, I would often joke with

Him, saying, 'Lord, I've cried so many tears that You must have run out of bottles to store them," Even in those hidden moments of pain, I knew He was with me, and I found comfort in His unwavering presence.

It's okay when your well of tears runs dry. It's okay when overwhelm leaves you unable to pray. It's okay when you feel like you can't take another step forward. Always remember God's love for you and that He will never leave you nor forsake you. His love runs so deep that He catches every tear you shed, storing them for eternity. That is the essence of unconditional love.

So what can you do in these moments? Pour out your heart to God—hold nothing back, for He can handle every raw emotion and unfiltered thought. After releasing everything within you, step back and allow Him to embrace and care for you. We often hesitate to share our deepest feelings with God, thinking it's disrespectful or inappropriate. But the truth is, He already knows what's in your heart; He simply wants to hear it from you.

Come as you are and speak from your heart. There is no protocol or proper etiquette required when talking to God. Release what burdens your heart and trust "Our Father who art in Heaven" to tenderly care for you in your time of need.

Heart Check-In

"You keep track of all my sorrows. You have collected all my tears in your bottle. You have recorded each one in your book." (Psalm 56:8)

I cried until my eyes were swollen, puffy, and red. I wept until I was bent over, doubled in pain from the ache in my stomach. I sobbed until the pounding in my head became so unbearable that I had to lie down just to keep from losing my balance. I bawled until there were no more tears left, emptied of everything but the silent cries of my heart.

Have you ever found yourself in a place like this? When the pain feels so overwhelming, and you wonder how to move forward?

For me, after my tears had run dry, I'd often find myself standing in the middle of the floor, hands on my hips, looking up to the heavens and saying, 'Lord, You must have run out of bottles to store my tears." The Word promises that He catches every tear we shed and records each one in His book. Imagine that—*every single tear,* collected and remembered. That's what I call unconditional love.

Knowing that He understands my every emotion and carefully catches each precious tear is the reassurance I needed to keep going. After reflecting on His love and attentiveness, I'd gather myself, wave my hand toward heaven, and say, "Alright now, Daddy, the ball is in Your court." It's my way of surrendering, knowing that He's already working on my behalf.

As I continued my faith journey, I knew that walking with the Lord didn't exempt me from daily challenges; my trust in Him was strengthened through each one. My usual routine was to wake up at 3:00 a.m., but this morning felt different. As I prepared for work, I remember telling the Lord, "I have no gas, and I have to get to work. You said to trust You, and that's exactly what I'm doing."

I buckled my daughter into her car seat in the back of my maroon GMC Envoy, started the engine, and took a deep breath. I prayed, 'Lord, if I run out of gas, so be it. I have no money, and I won't ask anyone for help. I'm trusting You to make a way."

TEARS OF FAITH

By the time I reached the corner, the gas gauge needle was well below empty. Still, I kept driving, each mile, a step of faith. About five miles in, as I merged onto the highway, I noticed the needle slowly moving in the opposite direction, creeping up past empty. Tears filled my eyes as I drove the 12 minutes to the babysitter and then continued on to work. Miraculously, the needle rose to about a quarter tank, just enough to get me through my day.

After work, I picked up my daughter and drove home. As I pulled into my driveway, the gauge was empty again. That night, I thanked God with everything in me, feeling held and sustained in His hands. I thanked Him for His favor, His provision, and His love for my children and I.

The next day was Wednesday, payday, and as usual, I started my morning routine. This time, as I headed out, I stopped at the gas station, feeling a deep gratitude for the One who'd carried me through. Tears of faith.

Time hadn't paused while I worked to navigate through life, trying to nurture my children emotionally, physically, and spiritually. Just as I struggled to stay afloat, God decided to throw another ripple into the waters, and I was left trying to keep from drowning.

CHAPTER 3

God Is Omnipresent - Talk To Him Often - At Any Time

My children are the heart of my world, and I've always tried to shield them from the heartaches; feelings of abandonment, rejection, and the inability to express themselves. Since the minute they were born, I've dedicated every waking moment to ensure that they felt loved, safe, and free from the emotional challenges I once faced.

From an early age, I made it a priority to instill in my children a sense of God's presence through practices like saying the Lord's Prayer before bed, expressions of love, daily affirmations, hugs, and family traditions that have strengthened my family bond. Even though we live in different states, we stay connected through a family chat and send each other a, "Good morning, I love you, have a wonderful day" text every morning. We also call each other throughout the week just to say, "I love you."

As I grew in my walk with Christ, I realized that the fears I once tried to shield my children from were emotional challenges I kept buried inside of me. Through open conversations, I learned that my children feel grateful for the life and love I've provided, and they've never felt the fears I once carried. They don't always walk the path I envisioned for them, and that's okay. I'm not God–only He knows their complete destiny. My job is to align with His plan and praise Him for creating my children for His glory.

What happens when my plan doesn't align with God's plan?

The Lord often wakes me in the stillness of the late-night hours. I believe it's because, in those quiet moments, my mind is free from the distractions of daily life. He knows that, during that time, He has my full and undivided attention. Throughout my walk with Him, I've felt His gentle whisper in my heart, saying, "When I wake you, praise Me." Being an early riser, I often find myself up before the sun, taking that sacred time to lift my voice in praise. These moments have become a treasured part of my journey with God—times to connect with Him in quiet reverence, seeking His presence and starting my day anchored in His grace. Although this sacred quiet time with God was a source of comfort and guidance, it did not fully prepare me for the next step in my faith journey.

In December of 2002, during the disharmony of my life, the Lord had welcomed me into ministry. He chose me as a vessel to share His word and preach the gospel to His people. This calling is a profound honor and a responsibility that I hold with humility and gratitude. I know that through His guidance, I am entrusted to carry His message of hope, love, and salvation to those who need to hear it. This journey of faith is one I embarked upon with reverence, eager to serve and to be used for His purpose. When my marriage failed, I struggled to understand why; I was emotionally worn out, embarrassed, ashamed and felt unworthy. But it was then that He shine His light on me. Despite the pain and confusion, I found a peace I couldn't explain—a strength that wasn't mine to begin with. In that moment, I chose to surrender, letting go of my own understanding. I answered the call God had placed on my life, knowing that He was guiding me through this season for a purpose greater than I could see. I stepped forward in faith, trusting His plan.

The next day, I called my pastor, Pastor Flowers, to share that God had called me to preach the gospel. His response was simple yet powerful, "Yes, I know. I've seen the anointing all over you for some time, but it wasn't my place to tell you—that is God's job." His words were both humbling and affirming, reassuring me that this call was truly from the Lord. After that conversation, things began to move quickly within the church, and I could feel God's hand guiding each step of the journey ahead.

I remember my first sermon vividly. In the days leading up to it, I cried and prayed, not out of nervousness, but because I dreaded being given a title. I wanted my ministry to be about serving, not labels. Titles felt like barriers, and I didn't want to be seen as *Sister Sheila, Missionary Sheila,* or anything else the church might choose. On that Sunday morning, I had an honest talk with Pastor Flowers, asking him to introduce me without a title. He graciously tried, but in the end, he still introduced me as a missionary.

As I embarked on the long walk to the podium, it felt like an eternity. I kept telling myself to let the introduction pass—but I couldn't. When I began to speak, I opened my heart to the congregation. With tears rolling down my cheeks, I explained that when the Lord speaks to me, He doesn't call me by a title. He calls me "daughter" or simply, "Sheila." I asked, out of respect, that they address me as Sheila, just as He does.

The Lord was moving swiftly in preparing me for ministry. I was soon given the honor of delivering the main message on a Sunday morning to the entire congregation. I fasted and prayed for days, asking the Lord to reveal His message, and He did. He gave me the subject, *Walls Around Your Heart,* a message that would be one of the most challenging I'd ever have to deliver. As I prepared, I realized that sharing this message would require me to open up about a deeply painful experience. Before I could deliver the message, there was one crucial conversation I needed to have. To be truthful, I needed to speak with Paul about a tragic chapter of my past—a terrible attack that had taken place 25 years earlier, when I was only 14. It was difficult, yet I knew that in revealing my own wounds, God could use my story to help others confront the walls around their own hearts.

When Sunday morning arrived, it was time to share the Word the Lord had placed on my heart. I remember seeing Paul in the back of the church, operating the audio equipment, watching me with protective eyes, ready to shield me if needed. I used a red styrofoam heart and several white bricks, to illustrate the message. I explained that when we're born, our hearts are pure, open, and unguarded. As we journey through life, facing hurt and disappointment, we begin to build walls around ourselves to protect against future pain. With each painful experience, these walls grow thicker, one brick at a time. Gradually, the white bricks of life encase our hearts.

I shared how, when we surrender to God, He starts to break through those walls, piercing them with His love, trust, and faithfulness. Slowly, His love softens and even disintegrates the bricks, bringing healing and allowing us to forgive. The past no longer has the power to haunt us, and as we heal, love and joy are restored in our hearts. I demonstrated this by removing each brick— *"betrayal," "disappointment," "abandonment," "rape," "low self-esteem,"* and *"loneliness"*—calling out its name as I did.

When I made my first altar call, I was overwhelmed by the number of women, both young and old, who flooded to the altar, carrying similar wounds. Speechless, I stepped aside and allowed the pastors to minister to His daughters as I wept.

In that powerful moment, I realized why the Lord had moved so profoundly in my life when I surrendered to Him at the age of 30. The first thing He asked me to do was write to my father, telling him that I forgave him and loved him because, as His Word commands, we are to forgive. I'm deeply grateful for God's hand over my life. Despite the incest and the trauma I endured, He spared me from a path of destruction. I could have easily found myself lost in a life of addiction, consumed by anger, or forever scarred. Instead, God took what was meant for harm and turned it into a testimony—a powerful story of redemption that I could share to help others heal.

Sometimes, true encouragement only comes when you've walked a similar path. I understand the struggles because I've lived through them. I am a living testimony of what God has done, what He is doing, and what He will continue to do—not only in my life but in my children's lives and for generations to come.

My faith was slowly increasing then, not just through Sunday sermons or reading scripture, but through the ups and downs, the valleys and mountaintop experiences I'd endured. My faith was growing because I was nurturing my personal relationship with God, spending intentional, intimate time with Him. I found strength in reading my Bible, meditating on His Word, and praising Him simply for being God. No requests or demands, just honoring Him for who He is.

As I watched the remaining bricks around my heart begin to crumble, I thought I had my path figured out. I was ready to coast through the rest of this Christian journey, feeling like I had reached a place of peace and stability. Oh, was I mistaken. Just as I was settling in, the Lord redirected my course entirely. He had a different plan in mind–a 2,500-mile journey across the country for my children and I. A journey that would take us far from California, never to return.

Cross-Country Journey on Faith

My divorce was finalized in 2005. As the judge asked if anyone contested, a small glimmer of hope lingered in my heart. Part of me thought we'd wake up from this nightmare and find the spark that once united us glowing brighter than ever. When the judge signed those papers, it was over. Through it all, there was no hate, disrespect, or malice between us—just acceptance that God, in His infinite wisdom, knew how every step in our journey would unfold. I always remind my children that I love them deeply. So much so that if I had to walk that path again so they could be born, I would do so gladly. God created them with a purpose, and I'm grateful He chose me to carry that seed. I smile at God's sense of humor, too—seeing their unique personalities and features, each a reflection of their parents.

In 2006, the Lord began preparing me to uproot my children and move us across the country to a city where we knew no one. I wrestled with God, asking why I needed to disrupt the stability I had worked so hard to create, especially after everything my children had endured over the past four years. The Lord made it clear, *"I need to isolate you so you can truly heal, because there's work for you to do in My Name. You need to trust Me completely—not in what you think the outcome should be, but in My plan. You need to rely fully on Me and not on your own strength."*

I began searching for a new home online. I desired a home in a safe, well-maintained, and diverse community. The home had to be two stories with all the bedrooms on the second level, a two-car garage, a front porch, and a backyard. I desired and expected this from God even though I had no savings and was living paycheck-to-paycheck. The constant stress of managing every penny, ensuring I tithed from each check, paying daycare, and sometimes not being able to buy the brand-name cereal for Monica made me feel like I was failing my children. She deserved the best, and as a parent, it was my responsibility to ensure she never went without. That was an internal battle I had to fight daily.

The reality was that, despite the financial strain, when people saw my children, they were always well-groomed, fed, and happy. I knew deep down that God would provide, although in my mind, His plan wasn't aligning with mine. I couldn't understand why it was so hard when I was doing everything right. I often reminded myself that God's plan was greater than my understanding, and in time, I'd see the beauty He was unfolding.

With Paul away at college, and Monica being bilingual, I needed to find a state with a good dual-immersion educational program. I started searching for homes in Texas. The Holy Spirit kept pointing me toward North Carolina. I focused my search on the city of Charlotte. I was getting close, but nothing felt like the right fit. Then, I stumbled upon Greensboro, a place I had never even heard of before.

When I researched schools, I found one that I preferred. Now that I had found a school for Monica, I reached out to the school board to inquire about the enrollment process. The responses I received could have been discouraging–they told me it was a lottery system, and I would be placed on a waiting list. I ignored these responses, because I knew without a doubt that the Lord had directed me to Greensboro and had already taken care of all the details. I knew this was the place; every time I tried researching other cities, roadblocks appeared. Calls wouldn't be returned, websites didn't work. The Lord had closed the door on every other option.

As I interacted with the North Carolinians, I asked for community recommendations. The responses I received were varied, but when I researched their suggestions, I knew it wasn't the right place for me. I had a specific vision and it was important that I committed to it. After months of searching, I was unsuccessful in finding homes that felt like the *one*.

One day, on my commute home, I prayed, "Lord, I know without a doubt that You've directed me to Greensboro, but I need your guidance to find the home you want me to live in. I'm frustrated because next year I'm relocating, but I don't know where yet. I'm stressed. Paul is away at college, and I'm commuting an hour each way to work while caring for Monica.

I'm involved in church, helping with the teenage ministry. There never seems to be a moment to breathe. I'm being pulled in multiple directions, and I feel overwhelmed." It was as if I had taken back some of the burdens I had already given to the Lord.

As tears streamed down my face, I kept praying, "Lord, I need you. I can't do this without you. Wherever you tell me to go, I'll go. Whatever you tell me to do, I'll do. Whatever you tell me to say, I'll say." That prayer was my act of total surrender, reaffirming to God that I was ready to follow His will without questioning it.

The next day, during lunch break at work, I found myself back online searching for homes. This time, I stumbled upon a new community. Up until this point, I hadn't even considered new construction, but something about it caught my attention. As I scrolled through the photos of the model homes, one in particular stood out. I kept going back to look at it over and over again, throughout my lunch hour. Eventually, I decided to email the builders, unsure of what might come of it.

The very next day, I received a phone call, and things began moving quickly. Despite not having any savings, I trusted the Lord. The process seemed surreal—papers were submitted, I was pre-approved, and everything flowed smoothly. My faith was strengthened as I saw how easy the online process was. I answered the pre-approval questions, and everything fell into place. No obstacles, no setbacks—just God's favor at work.

I began sharing my journey with others, hoping to inspire and ignite faith in them, sometimes the opposite occurred. Many people around me didn't understand why I was making such a bold move. I heard comments like, "You don't know anyone there, why would you go?" My response was always the same, "I know Jesus, and He's leading me there."

The whispers, the side-eye looks, and the doubts from others didn't faze me. Why? I knew what the Lord told me, and I was going to obey no matter what. Over the years, as I walked this path with God, I had seen my faith grow in ways I never imagined. There was no turning back now. With God leading me, I knew that this journey, though daunting, was part of His perfect plan for me.

I began searching for jobs within a 60-minute commute of the new community where we would be living. Over the course of four months, I diligently saved enough money for two airline tickets for Monica and me, as well as for a rental car, hotel, and meals for our trip to Greensboro. I booked our tickets for the second week of January in 2007. I was determined to sign the contract and start building our new home. Not long before our trip, I received an unexpected call from a university interested in interviewing me. The timing was perfect—it was for the same week I would be in Greensboro. I informed the university that I would be in town with my daughter for business, and she would need to accompany me to the interview. Everything seemed to be falling into place.

When it was time to reserve our hotel room, things took a turn. A major convention was taking place in Greensboro, and the hotel near the convention center was fully booked. Hearing that there were no rooms available, made my heart skip a beat. While there were other hotels in the area, safety was my top concern, especially since I was traveling alone with my young daughter. I was also accustomed to a certain standard of accommodations, which made finding the right place even more important.

I cried out to the Lord, asking for guidance. In an instant, a wave of peace came over me. I picked up the phone and called the hotel directly. The woman who answered was soft-spoken and kind, once again, I was told they had no available rooms. Curiously, she asked, "What is the purpose of your trip?" I shared my journey with her, explaining my faith, my move to Greensboro, and the steps I had taken to trust God through it all.

I could hear her typing on her computer, and after a moment, she told me, "I have one room available, but it's an ADA accessible room. Is that okay?" Without hesitation, I said yes. She then offered me the room at a lower price and explained the accommodations for an accessible room.

I thanked her profusely, and she replied, "I needed to hear your testimony. It encouraged me. I'm praying for you and your daughter, and may the Lord continue to bless you."

At that moment, I knew that God had worked through that interaction. Not only had He provided a place for us to stay, He also used my testimony to touch someone else's heart. It was another reminder of how He was guiding me through every step of this journey.

Heart Check-In

"For the Lord your God is he who goes with you to fight for you against your enemies, to give you the victory." (Deuteronomy 20:4)

Have you ever felt that the harder you try, that brick wall keeps getting higher and higher and you see no way of jumping over it? You feel like you're defeated. You think what's the use? There is no reason for me to keep trying. People are whispering behind my back. "Where's her faith now?"

You have to remember that there will always be people with no faith, standing on the sidelines waiting for you to fail. But you have to remember that God is with you. He has predestined your footsteps from the foundation of the earth. You have to remember that He created you with purpose and He is with you through every step of the journey.

You have to stand tall, hold your head up and thank God for fighting for you against your enemies. You have to speak life

> and positivity into each step. When you move the right foot forward, say, "Lord, You've ordained this step in my life and I know without any doubt that you're right beside me. I have no fear, just gratitude that you have given me the strength to move forward."
>
> I get bold with my steps and start telling Satan, "You're already defeated and have no power over me. God is with me, so I have the victory and you can't ever change that." You have to start speaking with authority and power because you have it.

The night before our flight, as I was packing, I grabbed my checkbook. It didn't have any extra funds, only what was budgeted for the trip, but I felt prompted by the Lord to leave it behind. I didn't understand why, but I obeyed.

This experience reminded me of the truth behind the phrase, *"obedience is better than sacrifice."* These words found in 1 Samuel 15:22, highlight the importance of following God's will with a sincere heart, rather than relying on outward actions or rituals. In this passage, the prophet Samuel confronts King Saul, for choosing his own judgment over God's explicit command to completely destroy the Amalekites and their possessions. The essence of this message is that God values our obedience far more than any ritualistic offering or sacrifice we might make. Sacrifice without obedience becomes hollow; true devotion is reflected in how we live, follow, and commit ourselves to God's guidance in our daily actions and choices. It's a reminder that God desires a relationship rooted in how we live and align our choices with His will.

In January of 2007, we arrived in Greensboro late in the evening. The next morning, I was preparing for my interview knowing that afterward, I'd be signing the contract to start building our new home. Monica sat quietly in the hallway while I interviewed, which went well. Afterward, we hurried back to the hotel, changed, and headed to the new community to view the model homes before signing. I had only seen pictures online, touring the homes in person, I remained drawn to the Patrick Henry model I had originally chosen.

As we reviewed our choices with the realtor, the agent asked for the earnest money, 1% of the purchase price of the home, to show serious intent to purchase. I remembered that God had told me to leave my checkbook at home. I explained that I didn't have it. To my surprise, the agent said, "That's okay, just sign here." It took all my strength to hold back tears. Tears of faith.

Before leaving the community, we visited our selected model again. Inside, we met a woman who worked at the university where I had interviewed that morning. She even knew the department I'd be joining. She confirmed that the community was highly desirable and mentioned that she wanted to buy a home there herself.

Shortly after returning to the hotel, the university called and offered me the job. While excited, I was concerned because the salary they offered wouldn't cover the mortgage. With faith, I explained my situation, saying, "I'd love to work for you, however, I need a salary that will allow me to pay my mortgage." They asked for my salary requirement, and after I gave a figure, they promised to get back to me. Within 15 minutes, they called again, offering my desired salary, though it would require a job title change and state approval, possibly taking up to 60 days. I agreed to the terms and accepted the offer.

Back in California, I shared my testimony with the church, praising the awesomeness of God and the power of trusting Him while stepping out in faith. Before the congregation on Sunday morning, I recounted the entire journey; the favor with the hotel room, the waived earnest money, and how the Lord even moved to change a state job title to bless me. Through it all, I reminded everyone that when you step out in faith, even when it feels like you're stepping out on nothing, you can still expect something with God's guidance.

Heart Check-In

Have you ever wondered why the people you support, encourage, and pray for, don't do the same for you? Do you ask yourself, "Why can't they be happy for me?" Many years ago when I was starting my Christian journey, I was excited although some of my friends and family weren't excited, instead they were pretty negative. I have to admit, it was like someone stabbing me in my heart. I kept thinking, "Why aren't you happy for me?"

Then I had a lightbulb moment, a sudden realization. Their unhappiness with themselves prevented them from ever being happy for me. What I needed to do was pray for them and continue moving forward.

How do you handle situations like this? Is it worth sacrificing precious moments of happiness to dwell on their discontent?

A couple of weeks later, I found myself telling the Lord, "I really want to pray over my lot before construction begins." Having only owned pre-existing homes, I always made a habit of walking around the property, praying for God's protection, peace, and presence. For this new home, I desired to bless the ground and every part of it, from foundation to rooftop, before any building began. The catch? I didn't have the financial means to fly back to North Carolina.

A few days after praying about it, I received an unexpected call from a Fortune 500 company inviting me to interview for a position I'd applied for previously. Amazingly, the interview was scheduled near my future home. Although I knew I'd ultimately be working for the university, I saw this as God's provision, giving me the opportunity to pray over the lot. The company arranged my flight into Greensboro, provided a rental car and hotel, allowing me to visit the property and pray over it before the interview the following day.

After accepting the terms, HR called back with an update: they'd found a cheaper ticket, meaning I'd now fly into Charlotte, drive straight to the interview, and leave immediately after. I was frustrated knowing I wouldn't have time to stop and pray over my lot, so I silently prayed for peace.

Later that evening, I received another call from HR. They were mindful of the three-hour time difference since it was 4 p.m. in California, and 7 p.m. on the East Coast. The woman explained that they'd missed the window for the cheaper flight and asked if I'd consider flying into Greensboro instead. I would then drive to the hotel near the interview and complete the interview the following morning. Afterward, I'd drive back to Greensboro, stay the night before flying home the next day.

I immediately agreed, and as soon as I hung up, I burst into praise. Not only would I have the opportunity to pray over my lot before construction began, but all my travel, accommodations, and meals were fully covered. God had truly provided!

Everything went as planned—I flew out, interviewed, and, unsurprisingly, I wasn't a fit for their organization. I knew the true purpose of this trip was the blessing it provided to pray over my lot. That afternoon, I stopped by the property, where the realtor provided a hard hat and an umbrella due to the heavy rain. Standing in front of lot #32, I watched as the red, muddy clay washed away into the street, carried by the rain to the sewer drain. At that moment, I like to think I prayed heaven down on that day. I prayed for every person who walked, worked on or near my lot, to be filled with His Spirit. I prayed that every hand, every piece of material, every nail, screw, piece of wood, and concrete poured would be anointed. I prayed that unspeakable joy would touch everyone involved in building my home. In Jesus' name, Amen.

On Memorial Day in 2007, Paul helped me move into a one-bedroom apartment, as construction on the new home had been delayed by three months. I was so grateful for his help, especially since my new job at the university started on June 1st. I had to wait two weeks before I could enroll Monica in a summer program. Paul arranged his internship plans in LA with consideration for his sister's daycare needs in NC, so I could start work. His support meant the world to me, and I couldn't have managed without it.

As construction progressed, we drove by every day to pray over what had been completed. The moment the frame went up, I was overwhelmed with gratitude. One day, while making our usual stop to pray before heading to the apartment, the Lord prompted me to teach Monica how to pray over the house. I took her tiny hands and placed them on each piece of wood, guiding her through the prayer. I prayed first, and then I asked her to pray. It was incredibly emotional to hear her, with such sincerity, say, "Bless this house, in Jesus' name." Then, she touched each piece of wood, saying, "Thank You, Jesus." Feeling God's presence in that act of faith and love is a moment I'd never forget.

Throughout this process, I felt like I was dreaming. My children saw firsthand the faithfulness of God. They witnessed how prayer could exceed anything we ever imagined. They watched as God turned a heartbreaking experience into something beautiful. Inside, my heart was overflowing with joy. I was blessed to hold my head high with pride knowing that my children saw the power of God reflected in a strong, faithful woman.

When the day of closing finally came, I was still in the dark about the costs. After numerous calls to the funding company, no one could provide me with an answer. My only available funds were from the paycheck I had received earlier that morning. I arrived at the closing location and waited there for hours, hoping for updates. Time seemed to drag, and for a moment, the "what-ifs" crept in, what if I didn't have enough for closing? What-if the bank wouldn't fund the loan?

I closed my eyes, whispered a prayer, and said, "God, You are in control, and I trust You. I give You praise because You're God." My heart raced as my name was finally called. I entered the room to sign the closing documents, and the lender asked if I had my cashier's check. I explained the situation, asking if she could please tell me the closing cost amount. She looked at me with empathy and apologized, saying, "Your closing cost is $326."

Tears started flowing as the weight of it all hit me. She asked if I was okay, and I nodded, quietly saying, "I'm just overwhelmed with joy right now." After a moment, I asked if I could go downstairs to the bank to get a cashier's check. She left the room, but when she returned, she said, "It's our fault, and we don't usually do this, but you can write a personal check instead."

I wrote the check, and after a brief moment, she handed me the keys to my new home. Overcome with gratitude, I picked Monica up from summer camp and then immediately called Paul to share the amazing news.

> Have you ever felt like God might not come through for you? Have you faced a situation where success seemed impossible, even with God? Maybe you couldn't envision the outcome because your logical plan didn't align with God's unseen path. Does that uncertainty stem from doubting God, or from not being in control? Does our need for control overshadow our faith?

Let's take a moment to reflect honestly on these questions. Everyone experiences moments of uncertainty, doubt, and wavering faith. And you know what? That's okay. We're human, and it's natural to feel a wide range of emotions. What truly matters is how we respond to those moments.

I believe that with each uncertain step, we're climbing higher, drawing closer to God in our spiritual journey. Through these experiences, God reveals powerful truths: He is in control, He is building our faith, and He is always present in every situation. These moments of weakness are opportunities to recognize Him as Jehovah Jireh—the Lord will provide.

Faith Walk During Unpredictable Time

In January of 2010, I began my annual 40-day fast, which I traditionally start at the end of one year, continuing into the beginning of the next. These fasts are my "I love You" fasts, where I dedicate the first few days to praying for others and then to spend the remainder of the time simply expressing my love and appreciation to God. In my earlier years, I would only drink liquids for 40 days, but over time, I transitioned to abstaining from both food and liquids from 6 a.m. to 6 p.m.

During this fast, the Lord gave me a vision—my employers at the university were sitting across from me at a table, informing me that they would no longer need my services. In the vision, I simply smiled and said, "Okay." From my walk of faith, I knew that when God showed me something, it was to prepare me for what was to come. The fast ended on February 10th, and I shared the vision with my assistant. She responded with doubt, saying, "Oh no, you really think that's going to happen? He (the director) is such a good person." I just smiled and said, "It's going to happen because God said so."

About two to three weeks later, my director asked me to carry out a task. I was to inform several students that they wouldn't be receiving their full scholarships for the semester. I declined, explaining that it was wrong to do this to students who depended on that scholarship, especially since it was the last semester of their senior year, and too late for them to find other funding. The discussion became passionate. There was no justification for this action. The students had upheld their part of the scholarship agreement with good grades, full participation, and the funds were available. I knew this firsthand because I oversaw this portion of the grant.

> Have you ever faced a situation where you were torn between doing the right thing and going along with an unfair plan just to be a team player? How do you reconcile your moral compass with the pressure to conform, especially when it negatively impacts people who don't deserve it? What if you prayed for guidance but didn't hear an answer from God? Would you stand in faith and choose the morally correct path?
>
> These are deeply personal questions that challenge us to examine our values and be at peace with the consequences of our choices. As Christians, I believe we're called to strive for what is right, even when the immediate outcome may not benefit us.

Looking back, I can see how doing the right thing brought its own rewards. The students I fought for graduated and went on to become professors, engineers, scientists, chemists, cybersecurity specialists, and other STEM professionals. More than a decade later, we still keep in touch, and I celebrate their accomplishments as they share their successes with me. Their journeys are a testament to the value of standing firm on our principles. For me, this was the reward for doing what was right—and it was worth it.

On March 10th, 2010, I was summoned to the director's office, where both the director and the professor of the program were sitting at the table. The vision I had received during my fast had come to fruition. I sat down, and the director began explaining that North Carolina was an at-will state, and that my role would no longer be funded by the grant. They handed me a letter stating that my employment was terminated, effective immediately.

When they asked me if I had any questions, I simply smiled and said, "No, I have nothing to say." The look of surprise on their faces was one of confusion. Separately, they each asked me if I had any questions, perhaps expecting a different response—maybe tears or pleading. But what they didn't expect was my calm demeanor. God had already equipped me with the step-by-step playbook, so I was ahead of the game. I had control over my emotions, and watching their confusion as I remained calm—the absence of crying, begging, or pleading for my job—was baffling to them. But it wasn't baffling to me. God had given me a profound sense of inner peace. I took the letter, stood up, and returned to my office to send an email to my students. In it, I expressed how proud I was of each of them, assured them they could reach out to me anytime they needed support, and informed them that, effective immediately, I would no longer be employed at the university.

I cherished the opportunity to interact closely with my students—a part of the job I truly loved and knew I would miss deeply. One tradition I started was giving each student a hug during their weekly check-ins before they left my office. With my own son away at college, I understood firsthand the longing for the daily hugs and the comfort they provided, which made this gesture even more meaningful to me.

For many of the freshmen, this was their first time away from home, and I wanted them to feel supported, not just academically but emotionally too. Over time, word spread, and

I began to notice students who weren't in the program, waiting outside my office for a hug.

I truly believe the Lord allowed me to comfort His people through these simple, yet anointed hugs. It was humbling to know that such a small gesture could provide so much reassurance, love, and encouragement to these young adults navigating such a significant transition in their lives.

I packed up my personal belongings and said goodbye to my assistant, who was in disbelief. As I left, I whispered, "Remember, I shared with you the vision the Lord gave me."

Later that year, the grant was not renewed, meaning the project did not receive a third year of federal funding from the granting agency. The Lord has a way of intervening when His people are treated unfairly.

Heart Check-In

"And the peace of God, which surpasses all understanding, will guard your heart and minds through Christ Jesus" (Philippians 4:7).

Have you ever been in an uncomfortable situation and everyone around you is waiting for you to fall apart and yet, you remain calm?

Before I became a Christian, if someone expected an emotional, erratic, or unprofessional reaction from me, I wouldn't give them the satisfaction. My reasoning was simple—to make it clear that I still held the upper hand. Petty? Perhaps, I'm just being honest.

Now, let's take a moment to reflect. Think about one of your own experiences. How would you have handled the situation

> before becoming a Christian? And how did your reaction change after the Lord revealed His playbook to you?
>
> This spiritual journey is rooted in unseen faith—a confidence that, even without tangible evidence, you know without a shadow of a doubt that God is leading you without any tangible evidence. When God is in control, failure is not an option.

That year, I was unemployed from March through December. There was no income coming into my household except from unemployment assistance and my inconsistent adjunct professor jobs. I earned enough to keep the mortgage paid every other month which kept me out of foreclosure. I alternated months, by paying the mortgage on even months and utilities and groceries during the odd months. My credit was shot and that stressed me out as I've always had impeccable credit.

During this time, I didn't reach out for state assistance. Psalms 37:25, *"yet have I not seen the righteous forsaken, nor his seed begging bread"* and as a daughter of God, I believed in scripture and wouldn't ask anyone for help. I knew my God was faithful and would not let me down. He did not say the road would be smooth. I know He is Jehovah Jireh (The Lord will provide) and that is enough for me.

We had made it through most of the year, though it wasn't without its struggles. Finances were extremely tight, but the Lord always provided for us. Despite the hardships, my church family never saw me show doubt or despair, but always heard me say, "I'm God's favorite child." December arrived, and there was no extra money to buy gifts for my daughter. The Christmas tree was beautifully decorated and festive but the gift boxes beneath it were empty. I remember crying out to the Lord, feeling exhausted and asking Him to bless us so that my daughter would have a couple of gifts to open on Christmas morning.

A few days later, I was talking to Paul, and he mentioned Christmas. I had never shared with him the financial struggles I was facing; I would always tell him, "The Lord sent us here, and He will take care of us." Without saying a word, my son, who was in graduate school at the time, said, "I gotcha, just tell me what you want to get Monica for Christmas." As I listed a few inexpensive items, tears rolled down my cheeks. Within a few days, I received a money order in the mail. I was so proud of him. He was becoming the man I raised him to be, a man who provides for his family with love and respect. He had the heart of a shepherd: protective, caring, trustworthy, knowledgeable, and a true leader.

For over 9 months, I had been struggling to find full-time employment. It wasn't for lack of effort, I had applied to hundreds of jobs, but nothing seemed to work out. One day, I was talking to a friend from Oklahoma about how discouraged I felt. She encouraged me to apply to HP (Hewlett Packard), as they were hiring. I followed her advice and submitted an application near the end of December. A couple of days later, Human Resources reached out to schedule an interview for December 31st.

At that point, I was exhausted and felt defeated. I remember standing in the middle of my bedroom, preparing for bed. Instead of my usual nightly prayers, I said to God, "I'm tired. I give my tithes, I serve You, I try to live a Christian life, but I'm tired now. I shouldn't have to struggle to pay my bills. I'm doing the right thing. You know me better than I know myself, and You know I could find someone to help with my bills, but I love You and I know You will take care of us. I'm tired." That night, I went to bed without praying for the first time in my adult life. I cried myself to sleep.

Have you ever faced a moment so discouraging that you threw up your hands and said, "I can't do this anymore. You win. I quit"? How did it feel to navigate that challenge? Did you find yourself questioning your faith or even losing faith in God? How did you rise above that discouragement?

Discouragement is a natural emotion, one that we all encounter at some point in life. It's okay to be honest with God about how you're feeling. Open your heart to Him and share your struggles. Remember, "The Lord is there" (Jehovah Shammah). He understands our pain and stands ready to guide us through with His unwavering love and compassion. You're never alone in those moments; God walks with you, providing the strength to rise

The next morning, still feeling discouraged, I got ready for the interview. By this point, I had been to so many interviews that I was just going through the motions. About 15 minutes before the interview, I stepped into the bathroom and suddenly blurted out, "Suddenly!" I repeated, "Suddenly!" and then a third time, "Suddenly!" It turned into a song, and I started singing, "Suddenly, suddenly, suddenly…" I felt a spark of excitement in my spirit, and my body began to move to the rhythm, as if I were listening to smooth jazz.

At that moment, the phone rang. It was the interviewer, letting me know that the company was closed for the holidays but expressing her desire to meet with me before the year ended. She began asking background questions, and when I told her I was from Detroit, the conversation took a personal turn. She was also from Detroit and asked which high school I attended. When I said Henry Ford High School, she laughed and told me her grandmother lived near there. We spent the next 15-20 minutes chatting about Detroit, connecting over shared memories and places.

Finally, she asked a few job-related questions before surprising me with a question about my desired salary. Not wanting to price myself out, I shared the amount I had been earning at the university. She replied, "That's good, but I'm going to start you with this amount instead." When she told me the salary, I was overcome with emotion–it was $25,000 more than I'd requested. She then asked if I could start on January 18th, 2011, since January 17th was Martin Luther King Jr. Day. The position was 100% remote. After the call, I wept with tears of joy, overwhelmed by God's provision and perfect timing. I kept thanking Him for His faithfulness and unexpected blessings. Tears of faith.

Heart Check-In

Have you ever felt hopeless? You've prayed, fasted and read your Bible, but still no answer from God.
- Everyone has experienced a state of hopelessness at one point in their lives. We're human and it's a part of our experience. The key is not to stay in that state of mind. Don't grow weary in seeking the Lord for an answer. He doesn't always answer when we want Him to.

What's next? How do I keep from sinking into a depression? How do I keep my faith? How do I keep smiling when I'm torn up inside?
- Keep seeking God through prayer, even if you don't receive an answer. Trust and know that He hears you. *"Therefore humble yourselves under the mighty hand of God, that He may exalt you in due time." (1 Peter 5:6)* Even during the moments when your insides are upside down with grief and hurt. Confuse the devil and reach deep into your inner-self and release the joy. You'll find that the more you allow yourself to smile, your joy will begin to bubble up to the surface. Before you

> know it, you'll be overcome with giggles and laughter…joy!
>
> Is it acceptable to be angry at God?
> - Some Christians might say, "Oh no, you can't get angry at God." They are entitled to their beliefs. But as for me, I believe in my heart that I'm God's favorite daughter and that our father-daughter relationship grows closer each day. *"God knew our thoughts from the beginning of mankind" (Genesis 6:5)*. So I don't have to pretend when He already knows. I have to be honest with myself so that I can express my feelings, thoughts, and everything in-between to my Father.
>
> When I have these moments I get real with myself, have a heart-to-heart conversation with God. After I've finished my pity party, I start to praise God for who He is. I tell Him how grateful I am that He created me in His image. Praising God will thrust you into a joy that surpasses all understanding when going through valley moments.

When Will The Layoffs Stop?

I thoroughly enjoyed my time at HP, where I experienced God's blessings and favor, especially when I led groundbreaking projects. As a Program/Project Manager, I oversaw a two-year initiative that was a first in the industry and has yet to be replicated. After working tirelessly to meet our deliverables, budget cuts came, and I was transferred to a different department. I spent about a year there before further cuts resulted in my layoff in July 2016.

Despite the uncertainty, I felt at peace. An emotion because of which, my coworker, Kristian, grew angry with me. We worked remotely, and though she lived about an hour away, we had become friends, meeting every few months for lunch. We worked closely during the layoff, making sure everything was in order. She had worked nearly 20 years at the company, while I had only been there for about four. Our severance packages were only at a $10K-difference. I knew that was God's favor, something Kristian, a fellow believer, understood as well.

I vividly remember that in the days leading up to the end of our employment, she called to check in on me. By nature, I'm a happy person and Kristian couldn't understand why I wasn't depressed. As a single parent and with Monica in high school, my circumstances seemed more challenging than hers—she was married with a stable income, and her daughter had graduated college debt-free. I reassured her, saying, "The Lord will provide as He always has."

Suddenly, Kristian became enraged, yelling, "You make me sick! You're always so peppy, you get on my nerves with that, you make me sick!" Then she hung up. I was heartbroken and cried for days, never knowing she felt that way. For years, I prayed for her, but we never spoke again. She cut me out of her life completely. I leaned on Ecclesiastes 3:1, trusting that people come into our lives for a season, and only God knows how long they last.

I didn't tell my children that I had been laid off for weeks—I didn't want them to worry. Since I couldn't collect unemployment until my severance pay was exhausted, I kept things to myself. I did share the news with my sister-circle, and Dee Dee immediately suggested we pray. As always, it was an anointed prayer. A couple of weeks later, Dee Dee called to check on me. She told me that she and Bishop had been praying for me. Then we chatted and laughed, as we always did.

As we were nearing the end of the call, Dee Dee kindly offered to pray for my situation once more. I responded, "No, don't pray for me."

She was taken aback, "What?" she exclaimed, her tone filled with shock.

I explained, "I've prayed, you've prayed, and Bishop prayed. I'm a child of God, and He heard our prayers. I've asked, and I don't have to keep asking. I don't have to beg God; He heard me the first time. I believe His Word, and I trust Him. So if you want to do something for me, just thank God with me."

She giggled and said, "Alright girl, amen."

That, to me, symbolizes true sisterhood; love, respect, and faith. It had been two months since the layoff, and I still hadn't found full-time employment. I've always had a backup plan. For several years, I worked as an online adjunct professor for three different universities. That extra income allowed me to take vacations with Monica and support her attendance at STEM (Science, Technology, Engineering, and Mathematics) summer camps, helping her prepare for college.

I had always said I trusted the Lord completely, and that was my heart's conviction. But now, He was about to test that trust. As I mentioned earlier, I had been laid off in July, and by September, things looked even more uncertain. As an adjunct professor, my work depended on course enrollments, and within weeks, all three universities informed me they had no opportunities available. For the first time, I found myself without a job and no backup plan, or unemployment assistance. I prayed, "Okay, Lord, I don't have a backup plan, and You're teaching me to rely on You, not on me, myself, and I."

I smiled and added, "Lord, You have a sense of humor, but I get it."

It was then that I realized that because of the purpose He placed in me before the foundation of the Earth, I must look to Him for everything, not relying on my opinions or backup plans. With tears in my eyes, I began to praise Him, and thank Him for simply loving me. "For I know the thoughts that I think toward you, says the Lord, thoughts of peace, and not of evil, to give you a future and a hope" (Jeremiah 29:11).

Mortgage Miracle

A few days later, I heard from my other sister-friend, Jan. She called me from Indiana to tell me about a program she had seen online that supposedly paid your mortgage. My immediate response was, "I never apply for stuff like that because it never works for me." Jan admitted she didn't know all the details but thought she'd share the information anyway. We chatted and giggled with girl-talk for hours before ending the call.

For a few days, I avoided looking into the information, convincing myself that I wouldn't qualify for these types of programs. Eventually, I decided to do my own research to make sure it wasn't a scam before contacting the organization. To my surprise, it turned out to be a legitimate organization. It took me three or four days to gather and upload all the requested documents.

Watch what the Lord does!

The organization contacted me after reviewing my application and told me I qualified for the program. They would cover my mortgage and Homeowners Association fees for 17 months. No lien would be placed on my property; I just had to agree to remain living in the home for seven years. If I decided to sell before then, I would need to repay a prorated portion of the mortgage to the organization.

After agreeing to the terms and signing the documents, I couldn't hold back the tears. These were tears of faith, flowing freely as I realized how faithful the Lord had been.

If anyone were to ask me the name of the organization, I honestly couldn't tell them. I don't remember it. All I know is that God provided. I never asked anyone for financial support, nor did I walk around complaining.

Touring Europe On Faith

During the last week of December, Monica and I, along with her school group, embarked on a 10-day trip to Europe, exploring Italy, France, and Spain. By that time, I had started receiving my unemployment benefits of about $300 per week. I was glad that I was blessed to have paid off the remaining balance of the trip with my severance package. The week before the trip, I said to her, "We only have $300 to spend. Everything is paid for, so there shouldn't be any extra expenses. You can buy a couple of things, but we need to be mindful that the $300 is meant to last us 10 days."

I didn't wave my hands to say, "Hey God, I'm going to need some extra money for this trip." Nope, I just thanked Him for the unemployment benefits, asked for safe travel, protection while we were in Europe, and blessings for everyone we encountered. I prayed that the memories we made with friends would be unforgettable. I never gave the finances a second thought because I had learned what it truly meant to trust the Lord wholeheartedly.

Now watch what The Lord did!

Just two days before we left, I received a check in the mail for over $3,000. It turned out to be a payout from a class-action lawsuit I didn't even know I was part of. I shared the unexpected blessing with my daughter, but told her, "We're going to stick with the $300 spending money we've budgeted for."

I was also able to give my tithes before we left and that felt like the cherry on top of the cake.

CHAPTER 4

Developing A Relationship With God

I thoroughly enjoyed our trip to Europe. It strengthened my faith and prepared me for the next phases of obedience in God's plan. Shortly after, I secured a 12-month contract position through a recruitment agency—an entirely new and challenging endeavor. The role came with a steep learning curve, and I struggled to navigate the nuances of their "system." Adding to the challenge, was a grueling 200-mile daily commute which called for early mornings, frequent gas stops, and parking fees.

Despite the distance, I firmly believed the Lord had opened this door and placed me there for a purpose, even while the purpose was unclear at the time. Friends and family often expressed disbelief about how I managed such a commute but my response was always the same, "the Lord sent me there for a reason."

During one particular 90-minute commute to work, I was utterly exhausted and struggled to stay awake. Gripping the steering wheel tightly, I turned up the radio and stretched my eyes as wide as I could, desperate to keep from falling asleep. Adding to the challenge was fog, darkness, and drizzling rain. Despite my efforts, I felt myself losing the battle. My eyes grew heavy, and I began to drift off.

Suddenly, the jerking motion of my head snapping forward woke me. At that moment, it seemed as though a deer was standing in the road ahead. Instinctively, I swerved to the right, narrowly avoiding a collision with an 18-wheeler. When I glanced in my rearview mirror, there was no deer in sight. The experience left me shook and puzzled.

It was a harrowing reminder of God's protection. Shaken to my core but resolute, I continued my journey to work. With faith as my anchor, I pressed on, trusting in His plan and finding strength in the belief that I was not alone on that road.

A few weeks into the role as an Information Technology (IT) project manager, another contract IT project manager, Debra joined our team. The recruiter introduced her to the team and assigned her to the cubicle to the right of mine. I immediately sensed she was my divine assignment. Every morning when she arrived at work, I would greet her with a smile and a warm, "Good morning." She seemed reserved, extremely quiet, and always focused on her tasks. My day typically ended an hour before hers, as I worked through lunch to leave by 3:30 p.m. to avoid traffic. Just before heading out, I would lean over and say, "Have a wonderful evening and a safe commute home." Debra would always smile and reply, "Thanks, you too." One morning, I felt compelled to share everything the Lord had placed on my heart for her. As I leaned in from the cubicle next to hers and spoke, her eyes filled with tears, and she whispered, "I had been praying about the very things you spoke." Overcome with emotion, my own tears followed, humbled by the privilege of being used by God.

That moment solidified my belief in following God's direction, regardless of inconvenience or naysayers. The assignment wasn't for them—it was mine, and being chosen by God is an honor. We never spoke of that moment again. Tears of faith.

Shortly after that encounter, my contract ended unexpectedly after just 30 days. There was no warning or indication of what was about to happen. One afternoon, the recruiter approached me with a security guard and asked if she could speak with me in the office. I calmly replied, "Yes, but you'll need to wait until I finish my project meeting." They stood behind my cubicle for 15 minutes until my call ended. Once finished, I got up and followed them into a vacant office.

The conversation was brief—over in about two minutes. The recruiter stated, "North Carolina is an at-will state, and the client will no longer need your services effective immediately. Do you have any questions?" I replied, "No," stood up, and returned to my cubicle to gather my personal belongings.

They trailed behind me as I packed up my belongings, and together we rode the elevator down to the lobby. As we stepped out, the recruiter glanced at me with a sly smirk and said, "Have a good day." I met her gaze with a radiant smile and replied warmly, "Thank you, and the same to you." With that, I walked out the door confidently, my head held high and my spirit unshaken.

I didn't question it. Instead, I felt a deep sense of peace knowing my spiritual assignment was complete. God had sent me there for a purpose, and I fulfilled it with faith, obedience, and a grateful heart without complaint.

> In Pentecostal circles, Christians often proclaim, "I will go where God tells me to go, do what God tells me to do, and say what God tells me to say." However, the reality is that this commitment often holds true only when it doesn't disrupt their comfort zone. Has God ever called you to do something, but you chose to ignore it because the timing wasn't right, it felt uncomfortable, or it didn't align with your plans? Most of us can honestly raise our hands and admit, "Yes, I've done that."
>
> As we grow and mature in our spiritual journey, our hearts and focus begin to shift toward full obedience to God's will. If you're not there yet, don't be discouraged—keep nurturing your relationship with God. In time, you'll find yourself walking in obedience naturally, without hesitation. And oh, what a joyous feeling it is to please God!

Some time passed, and I was able to secure another contract, this time about 20 minutes from my home. At first, it seemed ideal. By the end of the first week, I realized it wasn't the right fit. The organization was disorganized, overly focused on titles, and lacked a clear direction. Several project deadlines were missed, and there was no roadmap to outline goals, no milestones to measure progress, and no collaboration between teams. There were no recurring meetings with the project team, and no one could provide me with a clear scope or budget for the project. Still, it was a job, and I needed it to help cover monthly tuition payments.

At the start of my second week, I received a call from a recruiter about a project manager position with a construction company. I had no experience in construction, and the commute would be an hour each way. Despite my reservations, I agreed to attend the in-person group interview. It went well but I was left unsure if it was where I should be.

In the early hours of the morning, the Lord told me to take the position.

"What Lord? Are You sure? Why? Is there another assignment?" Questions swirled in my mind, God remained silent and did not offer any answers. Deep down, I knew I would obey His instructions whether or not I understood them.

The very next morning, while I was at work, the recruiter called. I stepped away from my cubicle to chat with her. She informed me that the president of the construction company wanted to meet with me one-on-one for a second interview. I agreed but explained that it would need to be after 5:30 p.m., as my current work hours were from 7:00 a.m. to 4:00 p.m.

That evening, I made the 1-hour drive to interview with the president of the company.

He asked me to develop a process, create the supporting documentation, and train his construction crew on various tasks and deadlines. The six-month contract he offered, however, came with an hourly rate lower than what I was earning in my current role as an IT project manager. Listening to the prompting of the Holy Spirit, I responded honestly, "I would like to work for you, but I can't accept a lower rate than I'm currently making."

He replied, "My employees don't make that rate, so I'm not sure if I can justify it with my business partners."

My response was straightforward, "I currently have a job just 20 minutes from my home, and this position would require a one-hour commute. My current role offers a higher hourly rate and a 12-month contract, compared to the six months you're proposing. I'd genuinely like the opportunity to work with you, but I would need the same salary I'm earning now. Please discuss this with your business partners, and let me know what you decide."

Then I stood up, extended my hand, and thanked him for the opportunity to meet with him again. You might wonder why I didn't ask for more money. The reason is simple: the Holy Spirit didn't lead me to do that.

By the time I arrived home, their recruiter called, offering me the position and asking me to start immediately. I responded professionally, explaining that I would need to give my current employer a two-week notice before making the transition.

The spiritual journey is often intriguing, challenging, and at times, completely illogical. On the drive home, I was certain the Lord had instructed me to take the contract. Yet, I kept reasoning with myself: this job pays the same rate, but the longer commute would increase fuel costs and vehicle maintenance, making it a poor financial decision. It didn't seem logical.

Have you ever made a decision that, in hindsight, didn't seem to make sense? Trusting God often means stepping into plans that don't align with our checklist or understanding. He sees the beginning, the middle, and the end, while we're called to simply walk in faith, focusing on Him. With each step, our faith grows.

When the assignment is complete, we often look back and chuckle, saying, "Oh, now I see why You wanted me to go this way." Too often, we overanalyze God's instructions instead of just obeying. Let's stop overthinking His ask, trust Him, and simply do what He's called us to do.

A couple of weeks later, I started my new role as a construction project manager for the company. It was a small business that had offices in two other states, and the employees were welcoming. It took a couple of months for me to train the construction crews across all three states and help them adapt to the new process. I created a step-by-step process on how they needed to perform their construction projects, outlining the timeline, specific tasks, and deadlines for completion. Essentially, I developed a construction project plan.

I never questioned the Lord about why He wanted me to take this construction position. I trusted that He had a purpose for me there. About four months into the job, I received a letter in the mail from the mortgage assistance program, asking me to call them. The letter didn't give any details, just a simple instruction to call the program coordinator. Naturally, my mind started spiralling. What if they decided to eliminate the program? If that happened, I wouldn't be able to pay my mortgage, and I still had about six months left on the program. On top of that, Monica's tuition was almost four times the amount of my mortgage, so I began to wonder what I would do in that case.

> **Heart Check-In**
>
> How to Handle "What Ifs"
>
> The phrase "What if?" often signals an internal battle between my heart and mind. My mind tends to spiral into uncertainty, imagining all sorts of scenarios, while my heart reminds me to put God first and trust in His guidance. Confronting these "what ifs" requires extra determination and strength. Though I don't think they ever fully disappear, I believe we can choose how to respond to them. As Proverbs 3:6 reminds us, *"In all your ways acknowledge Him, and He shall direct your paths."*

The next morning, I called the program coordinator. I learned that I needed a letter from my current employer verifying my employment and salary. This was part of the process to maintain eligibility after being on the program for a year. Without that letter, I would lose funding.

At first, my pride took over. I didn't want my employer to know that I was struggling to pay my mortgage or that I was receiving assistance. I reached out to Dee Dee again, to share. I remember saying, "I don't want people in my business like that." Her response was simple but powerful, "Honey, swallow your pride and tell the president what you need." I hesitated. *Let me think about it*, I told her.

There goes that pride again. I'm an extremely private person and asking for help felt like a big no-no. As I returned to my desk, I heard the Lord say, "I've given you favor with him, so tell him what you need." I went to the restroom and cried, overwhelmed by His goodness and grace, especially after I had let my pride get in the way.

The president didn't come into the office until the following afternoon. I asked if I could speak to him privately and we stepped outside, away from the thin walls of the small building. I shared my needs and the reasons behind them. Without hesitation, he responded, "No problem. Go inside and tell Drake what you need, and he will write the letter for you." Less than 30 minutes later, I had a signed document with the requested information. I emailed it to the program coordinator and uploaded it to their system.

At my previous contract job, this process would have involved multiple layers of management. But here, at the privately owned construction company, the president's office was just down the hall. Later that night, as I prayed, the Lord revealed to me that this was why He instructed me to take this contract position. *Tears of faith.*

"To obey is better than sacrifice" (1 Samuel 15:22).

One month before my contract ended, Karen, my Christian accountability partner, sent me a video of their Sunday service. When I watched, tears began streaming down my cheeks. Pastor Matt Keller of Next Level Church in Fort Myers, Florida spoke about God's faithfulness in tithing. He introduced the *90-Day Tithe Challenge* (90 Day Tithe Challenge - Next Level Church) inviting people to try God with their tithing, and if God didn't bless them, they would get their tithe money back. The verse he referenced was Malachi 3:10 which is a biblical principle for tithing, "Bring the whole tithe to the storehouse, that there may be food in my house. Test me in this," says the Lord Almighty, "and see if I will not throw open the floodgates of heaven and pour out so much blessing that there will not be room enough to store it."

I was facing numerous challenges with losing my job, working contract-to-contract, trying to pay tuition, and simply trying to survive. Despite all of this, I refused to ask anyone for assistance. I remember telling the Lord how guilty I felt for not giving my tithes and asking for His forgiveness.

Then, I watched the video of Pastor Matt.

He said, "Why should you tithe?"

For many, the idea of giving the first 10% of our income to the church can feel overwhelming. The thing is, it doesn't matter how much or how little we make, God promises to pour out blessings when we tithe. Tithing isn't just about the money, it's about training our hearts to trust God at His Word.

Pastor Matt continued, explaining how countless people experience God's blessings when they tithe, but that the hardest part is often the first step. That's why they created the *90-Day Tithe Challenge*. He said, "If you are not presently tithing and commit to giving 10% for 90 days, we guarantee that if God doesn't fulfill His promise of blessings, we will refund 100% of your tithe.

I had always been a faithful tither and generous giver, but over the last year, I couldn't give and it weighed heavily on me. I knew God understood, but tithing was my commitment to Him, and I felt like I had let Him down.

After watching the video, I reached out to the church in Florida. I wrote:

> *Hi, my name is Sheila McDaniel, and I live in North Carolina. My family attends your church, and they love it. I just heard about your 90-day tithe challenge. I'm a Christian and have been for 20 years. Over the past year, I've missed some tithing due to a job loss and other challenges. Please let me know how I can participate in the 90-day challenge. I don't care about the contract, I just want to tithe to your church for the next 90 days. Any pastor who gives his member a tithe contract is a pastor of great faith. Please follow up with me. God Bless.*

A couple of days later, the production director responded to acknowledge my email and let me know that he had forwarded my information to the operations team. Within a week, someone from the production team reached out with more details and instructions on how to set up online giving.

The enemy wasn't going to make it easy. Every time I tried to register for online giving, the system rejected me. Frustrated, I eventually contacted the production director for assistance.

I planned to give my tithes over Thanksgiving, unfortunately I hadn't registered in time. So, when payday came around again, I was overwhelmed by some financial pressures but determined to give. I reached out, asking, "Is there a number I can call to resolve this, or can someone call me?"

The production team called me, and after troubleshooting for a while, they couldn't understand what was going on with the online system, as they had never encountered this issue before. After a couple of hours, their amazing team managed to get me registered.

The Lord blessed me in just 30-days. In December of 2017, I received a check in the mail for thousands of dollars from a former employer in California that did not pay me the differential when they changed my job title. The second blessing was the extension of my construction contract. Although it was expiring in the middle of that month, the president asked if I could stay until January 5th, 2018 and I agreed. I had secured an interview closer to home for another contract as an implementation project manager for a lighting & fixture company. Once I interviewed with the company, they no longer wanted to hire me as a contractor but as a full-time employee. I started that role on January 15th, 2018. The third blessing was on January 10th when I received the check from the class action suit.

On Monday, January 15th, 2018, I emailed Next Level Church (NLC) about how the Lord blessed me in 30-days. Later that day, I received a response:

> Thanks for sharing your amazing story about the 90-day tithe challenge. It's incredible to hear how God has been providing for you and your family! We love to share stories like this to encourage others to trust God with their tithe! Would you be okay with us sharing a shortened version of your story during our weekend services and potentially on social media as well?

Of course, I agreed. On Sunday, January 21st, 2018, Karen called to share that Pastor Matt asked all three church campuses to pray for me. He only mentioned my first name but Karen knew it was me because I had shared my testimony with her as accountability partners do.

On February 18th, 2018, I emailed Karen again.

> I'm glad we're accountability partners! I wanted to share how the Lord is continuing to bless me since accepting the 90-day tithe challenge. It hasn't even been 60 days, and He's showering me with blessings over and over again. I was excited to receive my first paycheck from the lighting & fixture company on February 2nd and as soon as I arrived home I immediately sat down to give my tithes. Giving my tithes is a personal commitment that I choose to do with every financial monies that I receive is a feeling of love that I'm giving to God. Imagine that you're walking through a beautiful field of bright yellow flowers that doesn't exist on earth, and you're holding God's mighty hand, smiling, talking, and enjoying time with her daddy. Well, that's the image and feeling that I have when I give my tithes.
>
> You already know about the new job that started on January 15th, so let me start from the beginning…"

Tithe giving:

- *December 11, 2017 - I gave my first tithe challenge (this was from a bi-weekly paycheck)*
- *December 15, 2017 - I gave my tithe from a financial blessing*
- *December 23, 2017 - I gave my tithe from a bi-weekly paycheck*
- *January 5, 2018 - I gave my tithe from a bi-weekly paycheck*
- *January 10, 2018 - I gave my tithe from a financial blessing*
- *January 19, 2018 - I gave my tithe from a bi-weekly paycheck*
- *February 2, 2018 - I gave my tithe from my first bi-weekly paycheck of new job*
- *February 2, 2018 - I gave my tithe from a financial blessing - this was a different financial blessing*
- *February 6, 2018 - I gave my tithe from a financial blessing*
- *February 7, 2018 - I gave my tithe from a financial blessing*
- *February 8, 2018 - I gave my tithe from a financial blessing*

I'd been paying Monica's college tuition through a four-payment budget plan each semester. This spring semester, from January to April, I planned on making a sizable payment. I did this so she wouldn't end up buried in student loan debt. That said, I was living off credit cards—making the payments just so I could turn around and use as much of it as possible to pay the bills. It wasn't ideal, but I was grateful that the Lord made a way when it felt like there wasn't one.

Just when I thought I couldn't handle another setback, I got a call from the bank, threatening to repossess my car. I had a few months left on the loan. That night, I was really stressed. As I stepped into the shower, I started praying, and by the time I finished, I felt the stress fade away. Prayer is a powerful tool. It taps into the innermost realm of God's presence. When I pray, I'm able to be open, honest, and vulnerable while trusting that God is there for me. When I pray, I'm giving everything—the hurt, disappointment, stress, weakness, and things that I don't understand to God. Prayer is powerful and you can pray in your own unique way. That day, I simply started thanking the Lord for my joy and smiled.

Later that night, the Lord woke me up, and I found myself praying in tongues. I couldn't stop. This went on for a while. Then, on Tuesday, I received a financial blessing deposited into my checking account from monies that were owed to me. Wednesday brought another and on Thursday, I received another. On Thursday, I was standing in line at the grocery store. It took everything in me not to break out and start praising the Lord right then and there.

I praised Him all the way home and couldn't wait to sit down at the computer to give my tithes. Then, I paid the required amount to bring all my car payments up to date. I couldn't stop praising Him! *Tears of faith.*

> **Heart Check-In**
>
> Everything you're faced with is preparing you to step into the promises God has for you. Through the trials, the storms, the stresses, and the struggles, God has seen your faithfulness. He's witnessed the sacrifices you've made, the tears you've cried, and the effort you've poured into trusting Him. He knows the pain caused by others and the resilience you've shown in pressing forward. This is not the end—it's a divine setup. Keep your head high, stay steadfast, and keep walking. The same God who brought you through the fire is leading you into the fulfillment of His plans for your life. The promise is ahead, and He's with you every step of the way.

After taking the 90-day tithe challenge with Next Level Church (NLC) in November 2017, I finally had the opportunity to visit the church in-person in December 2024. I made a whirlwind 24-hour trip to Fort Myers, FL, specifically to meet Pastors Matt and Sarah Keller. Meeting them was extraordinary—their down-to-earth nature and approachability exceeded my expectations. Karen facilitated introductions, and we commemorated the moment with selfies.

From the moment I pulled into the parking lot, the atmosphere was charged with genuine love and spiritual energy. Everyone extended warm hugs and greetings, their smiles radiating what felt like divine light. The sound of children's laughter and excitement as they entered the building added to the joyful environment. Pastor Sarah delivered an energetic, Spirit-filled message during the Sunday morning service.

Afterward, Karen and I drove to NLC's second location where I attended their three-hour Empowerment Track session. NLC describes this program as being "designed to accelerate us into full engagement with Jesus and His purpose for our life. If you're new to Next Level, your spiritual growth has plateaued, or you just need a little help finding what your next step is, this group is for you. The Empowerment Track was designed to help each one of us become more fully engaged followers of Jesus regardless of the season we are walking through."

In small group discussions, we explored the church's history. The pastors' transparency about their personal lives and spiritual journeys made the experience especially meaningful. I gained a deep appreciation for NLC's impact not just in their city, but throughout their state and globally. I haven't felt this level of excitement about church involvement in years—even recounting the experience fills my spirit with joy. I remain committed to tithing to NLC until divine guidance directs me otherwise.

CHAPTER 5

Your Heart's Desires Come With Faith Challenges

I've shared the challenges I faced in ensuring Monica graduated debt-free. This goal was deeply personal, stemming from my own experience of earning several degrees without financial support from my father, despite his ability to assist. I'm grateful to God for blessing me with the ability to complete my education without debt, and I desired the same for my children. To pay for Paul's tuition, I refinanced my home in California and used the equity on top of taking out parent loans. I've always believed that knowledge is invaluable—something no one can take away. I made it a priority to instill in my children the importance of putting God first, embracing education, living with honesty, working hard, being financially responsible, upholding respect and integrity.

To ensure Monica wouldn't carry the burden of student loans, I worked multiple jobs and endured mistreatment from employers while prioritizing her education. I wanted her to start her career without the weight of debt hanging over her for decades. As a parent, I felt it was my responsibility to prepare my children to lead productive, successful, and honorable lives. Watching both walk across the stage to receive their bachelor's and master's degrees was a profound validation of my efforts and a testament to their preparation for success.

Lord, I Can't Handle Anything Else

TEARS OF FAITH

The time had arrived for Monica to start her freshman year at Virginia Tech. A few weeks before freshman move-in, we learned she would need a special laptop for her engineering program—one that cost almost $3500. We had the option to pay half the cost to reserve it, with the balance due on move-in day. Unfortunately, I didn't have the funds for the down payment. Paul stepped in and used his credit card to reserve it for her. I was grateful, but my pride reared its ugly head again. As a parent, it was my responsibility to handle those expenses. Although I smiled on the outside, inside I was crushed, thinking, *You need to step up your game, this is your responsibility.*

A week before move-in, I received a call from my daughter—she had been in a car accident while shopping for her dorm items. The same GMC Envoy from California, which God had provided me with gas to drive to work when I couldn't afford it, was wrecked. She was distraught, I kept asking, "Are you okay? I couldn't care less about the truck. I'm just thankful that you're safe." I instructed her on what to do, reminding her not to say too much to the police officers.

As I was speaking to her, I totally forgot I was at work, training Jim, a construction worker, on new processes. After I hung up, Jim, having overheard my call, asked if she was okay. I assured him she was, and he began offering advice on dealing with the insurance company. It was helpful, and I realized how often the Lord places people in our path to guide us.

I completed my training session and left work early, driving to the dealership where my truck had been towed. As I cried on the drive, I whispered,

> "Lord, I know you got me. You are my strength, and I'm your favorite daughter. I know I'll face many trials, but I will conquer them in Your name. I know that all my tears are stored in jars in heaven, and you are always with me. I will go where you tell me to go, and do what

You tell me to do. I will praise You in the good times, and the challenging times. Lord, you are my everything, and I can't do this without you."

When things become overwhelming for me, praising and worshipping God brings calmness, and inner peace within me.

When I arrived at the dealership, I asked for the keys to my truck, to gather my personal belongings. As I was doing so, a young mechanic approached me. He said, "Ma'am, they're going to total your truck because it would cost more to repair it. It's an older model, so it's easier for them to deem it as a total loss." I felt the weight of everything on my shoulders. In my mind, I thought, *Lord, now I need to come up with money to rent an SUV to travel to another state and move my daughter into her dorm in just a few days.* The young man, noticing my frustration, stated, "I used to work for an insurance company as an adjuster. I can tell you how the process works. You don't have to accept their first offer." He gave me advice on what to expect from the insurance adjuster, how to prepare my list of questions, and how to negotiate a better settlement. He handed me his business card in case I needed help later.

Overwhelmed and determined, I held it together because I couldn't afford to fall apart. Monica was counting on me. I knew the onlookers and naysayers were waiting for me to break.

Heart Check-In

Have you ever felt overwhelmed?

There are times when the weight of overwhelming thoughts and emotions tries to capture, torture and defeat us. In those moments, we can become stubborn, determined, and prideful. We tell ourselves that the onlookers and naysayers won't have the last laugh. We know that God is with us, and that He is

> our strength. We must remind ourselves to put aside the "woe is me" mentality and focus on Him.
>
> "I can do all things through Christ who strengthens me." (Philippians 4:13)
>
> I recite affirmations to myself, "Lord, I love you and will do what You tell me to do, go where You tell me to go, and say what You tell me to say. Why? Because You created me, and You are with me and failure isn't an option."
>
> It's okay to feel overwhelmed for a moment, you can't stay down. Get up, dust yourself off, and get back in the spiritual race. We're human, made of flesh and blood, live in this earthly realm, therefore, feeling overwhelmed is part of the journey. Remember, we have the most powerful weapon in the universe on our side…Jesus! We must remember who our Father is…Jesus! Go ahead, say, *I can do all things through Christ who strengthens me.*
>
> Now start walking in your strength.

I followed the instructions I was given. I researched and found three vehicles of the same year, make, and model as my GMC Envoy. I called each place directly to verify the prices listed online and documented the information. I even printed the advertisements. When the insurance company made a low-ball offer, I countered by requesting the names and addresses of the dealerships they were using for their valuation. They sent me three with contact information, but upon reviewing them, I discovered that two of the dealerships were out of business, and the third didn't have any similar vehicles on their lot. In addition, all three estimates were two years old.

I was grateful for the people the Lord had placed in my path to guide me through this process. Armed with this new information, I called the insurance company back within the hour, explaining that their estimates were fraudulent. I demanded a fair settlement and insisted on receiving a check by the next day. At first, they refused, I informed them that I would file a complaint with the North Carolina Attorney General's office, share my experience on social media, and contact local news stations. Reluctantly, they agreed, and the check was FedExed to me the following day.

The check arrived the day before we drove to Virginia Tech located in Blacksburg, Virginia. The bank placed a hold on the check. I rented an SUV, and we packed her belongings into the truck, departing before sunrise. I only had $100 cash and about $500 available on my credit card. We arrived at the dorms early. The energy was electric as freshmen and their families arrived with trailers to unload for move-in day. We made several trips from the curb, hauling boxes up three flights of stairs to her dorm room.

I was so proud of her. Proud of her drive and determination to pursue her dreams. We organized her room, lofted her bed, then took a break to pick up the laptop, and pay the remaining balance. I lacked sufficient available funds on my credit card, and the insurance check had not yet cleared. Once again, Paul stepped in to cover the difference. The bond between my children and me is unbreakable and full of love for each other. I'm deeply grateful for that connection. With the laptop in hand, I finally felt a sense of relief, knowing she'd be set for the next few weeks. Tired and exhausted, I had to leave by 5pm because I didn't want to drive 2.5 hours in the dark, afraid I might fall asleep behind the wheel. *Tears of faith.*

God Was Up to Something

I finally landed a long-term contract as an IT infrastructure project manager just 20 minutes from my home. Finally, I would have a steady income—enough to ease some of the weight of tuition payments, paying down my credit card balances, and rebuild my credit. I've always had impeccable credit and taught my children to be good stewards of their finances. I was beginning to see a glimmer of light peeking through the clouds with this new contract. Hold on, God was about to throw a pebble into the water to create a ripple. Six months into the role, I received an email from a recruiter.

On Friday, October 5th, I received an email from a financial talent acquisition recruiter. I glanced at it and continued working, not thinking much of it. About 10 minutes later, I received a phone call from an unfamiliar number. Normally, I wouldn't have answered, and I'm not sure why I decided to pick up. The voice on the other end identified herself and mentioned that she had just sent me an email. She explained that my resume was given to her by Regina, a senior vice president who thought I would be a good fit for the process design consultant position. Then she asked if I had any questions, to apply online if I was interested, and to call her afterward. I said, "Okay," and moved on.

I didn't give the conversation much thought and went about my day. I figured, *Whatever, I don't know a Regina at that company.*

On Tuesday, October 9th, the recruiter called again, this time at work. She gave the same introduction about Regina passing along my resume. At that point, I decided to lay out my terms.

"I can't accept less than this dollar amount," I said.

She replied, "Is that your salary expectation?"

I responded, "No, that's hourly." I was still thinking this was a contract role. She did the math and said, "That's a little higher than the position's range, but it might be negotiable."

She started telling me what great benefits the financial institution offered. I explained, "My daughter is in college, and I must pay both tuition and a mortgage. I can't take anything less than this dollar amount."

Finally, it clicked–this wasn't a contract position but a full-time, permanent role.

The truth was, I had been praying for a permanent, full-time job and thanking God for the position for a while. I usually pray and ask God for something once or twice. After that, I begin thanking Him, because I know He heard my prayers and that He will bless me in His timing. I have the faith to believe it and thank Him for it, even though it hasn't manifested yet.

I remember talking to the Lord about my current contract position, saying, "Lord, I'm grateful for the job you've blessed me with. I'm very thankful, however, I really want something permanent, something stable."

Later that evening, I decided to look Regina up on LinkedIn. To my surprise, she *was* a senior vice president. That piqued my curiosity. Maybe I should apply, I thought. I went online, filled out the application for the Process Design Consultant position, and hit "submit." To be honest, I really didn't read the job description. By the time I finished, it was around 10 p.m. and I knew the recruiter would not be in her office. I still called, left a voicemail, and sent an email as she instructed.

The next day, on Wednesday, October 10th, I received an email from another recruiter at the same company. She offered several dates and times for a 30-minute phone interview. I selected three options, and within 20 minutes, I had a confirmed interview for

TEARS OF FAITH

Monday, October 15th, at 8:30 a.m. Things were moving so quickly that I didn't take time to evaluate what was happening.

Over the weekend, I glanced at the job description for the upcoming interview.

On Monday, October 15th, I found a vacant conference room to interview with Regina, who had been with the company for 31 years, and Susan, a senior vice president with 39 years of experience. They didn't want to know about my project management skills–they were already impressed by my resume. They focused on my experience with process mapping, design, creation, and procedure skillset, which I happily elaborated on.

At the end of the interview, Regina asked me how I found out about the position. I thought, *Really? You gave my resume to the recruiter!* I figured it was a test to see if I'd tell the truth. So, I said, "I periodically check your company's website for job postings. However, for this particular position, your recruiter called me." I couldn't remember her name, so I mentioned that, and Regina guessed, "Was it Tiffany?" I responded, "It could be."

After the interview, I followed up with a thank-you email, mentioning the recruiter's name. To be honest, it wasn't one of my best interviews. Oh, but God!

About an hour later, the recruiter called to check in. She mentioned there were other candidates, and it would be a couple of weeks to finish interviews. If I was successful, the next step would be a face-to-face interview. I simply said, "Okay," and didn't think about it much more. If it was meant to be, it would happen.

The following day, I received another phone call from the recruiter. I stepped into a vacant conference room to take the call. She asked if I was still interested in the position. I said, "Yes." She confirmed my salary requirements and reiterated that it was a little higher than the salary range, and promised to check with the hiring manager. About two hours later, she called me back to ask if I was still interested. "Yes," I confirmed, a little puzzled.

Then she asked, "I'd like to officially offer you the position with your desired salary. Do you accept?" I replied, "Yes, thank you."

She told me my title would be Vice President, Process Design Consultant, and the salary was exactly what I asked for. She also mentioned four weeks of paid vacation, ten sick days, a 401(k), and a whole lot of other perks. She said I wouldn't receive a bonus in 2019 because I had just started. I was overwhelmed with gratitude to the Lord, struggling to keep my composure. Tears of faith.

Everything happened so quickly. I received my offer letter on October 18th. When I arrived home that evening, I spent two hours filling out the background check forms. I was scheduled to start on October 31st, contingent on the background check clearance.

Stepping into my new workplace that morning, I felt a surge of relief wash over me. The promise of comprehensive benefits meant more than just healthcare—it represented the ability to provide for Monica's education and our future. Though not all my worries disappeared as I walked through those doors, the burden I'd been carrying suddenly felt more manageable.

At security, I was told to wait a little longer for someone from my team to meet me. That raised a red flag in my mind. As I followed Alice, the young lady who would show me around, I noticed a lot of people working in a call center setting. When we reached the back of the building, they still hadn't assigned me a desk or equipment.

After what seemed like hours, Shelby, my manager, arrived at work. She introduced herself and said I would need to sit in the open area with the call center agents as there were no available offices. I took it in stride, thinking, *I'm here for my daughter's tuition, so I'll deal with it.*

Shortly afterward, a young Black woman arrived and sat in the cubicle across from me. She introduced herself as Belinda. I told her that I just started, and I didn't have a desk or any equipment yet. She placed her personal items in her desk drawer, locked it, and asked me to follow her. She assisted me with getting all my access and my equipment. We became friends, and I'm forever grateful for her support.

That afternoon, Shelby called me into her office to introduce me to the team over Zoom. I stood awkwardly, as she insisted they get a good look at me. I felt uncomfortable, like I was being auctioned off. It was so humiliating. The team introduced themselves, and then the questions came. "Do you have any children? Are you married? How long have you lived in Greensboro?" All I could do was smile and share that I had two beautiful children that God has blessed me with. I couldn't figure out why they were all fascinated with me. As I stood there, it became clear–there was no one on the team who looked like me. *Is that why they had so many questions?*

I pushed those thoughts away, telling myself, *It's about the tuition money.* The majority of the team was really nice, and I tried to focus on that.

After a couple of months, I joined a volunteer group for veterans, MSAG (Military Support and Assistance Group). I met many wonderful people, some who would later have influential roles in my career. We volunteered at schools, assisting veterans and their families throughout the state. I was never starstruck by someone's position and title, I always looked at them as normal people.

The Lord was putting me in the presence of influential people. In a notable development, the Chief Diversity & Inclusion Officer, a Black woman, who took the initiative to meet with me, reached out to introduce herself. A few days after the meeting I was summoned to Shelby's office. Her response was stern and dismissive: "You need to get somewhere and sit down. You haven't been here long enough to talk to executives." Attempting to bridge the gap professionally, I asked if she would consider mentoring me. Instead of addressing my request, she simply repeated her earlier statement about staying in my place. I thanked her politely and returned to my desk, grappling with a mix of confusion and disappointment over the interaction.

When Belinda arrived, I asked her if we could take a walk, and she agreed. She began to explain the culture of our workplace. I limited my volunteer hours and focused more on surviving at work. Soon after, I was given another manager, Bill, in project management. Project management wasn't the role I accepted, and for three months, I kept asking to be placed back in process design. I had to file a complaint with Human Resources (HR) before I was placed back into that role. The HR representative said, "off the record, be extremely alert as they didn't want to comply with my request and will probably make it difficult for you."

Every morning when I arrived at work, I would always greet everyone with a cheerful, "Good morning." One day, an associate asked me, "Sheila, why do you talk to us?" I was taken aback. "What do you mean?" I asked. She replied, "You're a vice president, and VPs don't talk to us." Before I realized it, my response was, "That's the stupidest thing I've ever heard." People are people, and titles don't make a person better than anyone else. The next morning, as I made my way to my cubicle, I did what I always did. I greeted everyone with a "Good morning." This time, something miraculous happened. The associates replied, "Good morning." From that moment, I formed a bond with most of them. They were more than willing to assist whenever I needed it, and I got to know them beyond a professional level.

On the other hand, my new process design manager, Lisa, was anything but warm. She didn't like the fact that HR put me on her team, and every day felt like a living hell. It was a brutal and toxic environment. I remember praying, asking God what was going on. I said, "God, you blessed me with this job, I didn't go looking for it." The Lord said, "I put you there to stir the waters." I remember bending over and weeping uncontrollably saying, "I don't want to stir the waters. I just want to go to work and come home. I didn't ask for this." His only response was, "I'm with you."

I cried until my stomach ached and I had a headache.

Heart Check-In

Have you ever found yourself in a situation you didn't ask for? What do you do when the Lord says, "I put you here, and I'm with you?" Does that make you feel better?

As long as we have breath in our bodies, we will be placed in uncomfortable situations. Does it feel good? Absolutely not. Our feelings don't dictate God's purpose for us. The discomfort doesn't disappear just because we don't like it. What matters most is our attitude in the midst of it. Will you whine about it, knowing it changes nothing? Or will you lift your hands and thank God for choosing you to walk through this fiery path?

After, we cry and throw temper tantrums, reality sets in. We still must walk through the uncomfortable path, now or later. Either way, we have to face it. We need to remind ourselves of Jeremiah 29:11, "For I know the plans I have for you,"

> declares the Lord, "plans to prosper you and not to harm you, plans to give you hope and a future."

The tension at work grew to be unbearable. It got to the point where I would complete my process designs, only to have a peer present the work as their own. Lisa would give them raving reviews, and when they told her I did the work, she still refused to acknowledge me. Frustrated, I began to search for other roles within the company. Every time I spoke with the hiring managers, they would tell me that they wanted to hire me—only to say they needed to reach out to my current manager, Lisa. After a few potential roles fell through, I realized she was blocking my transfer.

One day, on a Zoom call, something unforgettable happened. While Monica was home on break, she stood in the doorway of my home office and overheard Lisa calling me "dumb" and "stupid" in front of my peers. Tears rolled down my cheek, and when the call was over, she asked, "Are you okay?" I replied, "No." Monica stood frozen in shock, unsure of how to respond. It was the most humiliating moment of my life, the first time Monica saw me vulnerable, and helpless. In that painful moment, something shifted in her. She began to understand the depth of my love, realizing I was enduring this mistreatment because I was doing everything I could to pay her college tuition.

The final straw came during my end-of-year performance evaluation. I refused to sign it because I disagreed with the assessment. Lisa was furious and had HR join a call, trying to pressure me to sign it. I stood my ground, knowing it was my right to disagree. In response, I filed a formal complaint with the Equal Employment Opportunity Commission (EEOC). Throughout it all, I kept asking God, "Why?" He did not respond, I knew He told me months before that He put me there to stir the water. So, like a good soldier, I endured the emotional pain.

After I filed my initial complaint, Lisa's response was swift and severe. Although the EEOC had assured me that retaliation was prohibited, the very next day Lisa unleashed the fiery, fierce, fury of hell upon me as a direct result of my complaint. This prompted me to file an additional retaliation complaint with the EEOC. Months later, when mediation was arranged, the financial institution came prepared with legal representation. Despite their attempts to negotiate my resignation with a compensation package, I stood firm in my position, knowing I had acted appropriately throughout the situation. Also, God hadn't instructed me to resign or accept their compensation package, so I stood still.

About two weeks after the mediation, Lisa began offering to help me find another position within the company. With my guard up, I pretended to accept her assistance, but continued applying for jobs without sharing those postings with her. I applied for a Cyber Security Technology Technical Project Manager position and interviewed a few days later. The interview went well, and HR reached out with an offer. I chatted with Amanda from HR about the salary, which appeared to be a lateral move, and I was fine with that. However, she advised me that, based on the tier schedule, my salary might be higher. She asked me for a couple of days to complete her analysis and submit it for approval.

When I heard back from Amanda, she informed me that the salary had been approved, and she was preparing the offer letter. During our conversation, I learned that Amanda was also a fellow believer, which deepened our connection. She shared that securing the approval had been challenging, but it was worth the effort. I expressed my gratitude, telling her that I had been praying for the right opportunity and thanked her for her role in the process, which I attributed to God's guidance. Amanda agreed, saying she felt blessed to be part of His plan. She even shared a scripture, Psalm 31:14, *"But as for me, I trust in You, O Lord; I say, You are my God,"* that she found particularly fitting for the day. I shared my own testimony, referencing Deuteronomy 28:2, *"And all these blessings shall come upon you and overtake you, because you obey the voice of the Lord our God,"* and how God's blessings had overtaken me through her actions. Amanda revealed that her decision to advocate for a higher salary was divinely inspired, as she would normally have processed it at a lateral rate. She felt led by God to take extra steps on my behalf. We both recognized His work in the situation, shared mutual appreciation for each other's faith, and agreed to stay connected.

When I logged in at work the next morning, my offer letter was waiting for me. I read it and accepted. *Thank you, Lord!* I was walking on clouds all day.

A couple of days later, in the late-night hours, the Lord woke me up and said, "I've moved you out of the water onto dry land. I have plans for you." I couldn't go back to sleep as I was up praising Him! The storm was over, and I had made it to the other side. *Tears of faith.*

Two weeks later, I started my new role, and it was great! This was a great year! In April of 2022, I made the last tuition payment, and my daughter graduated with her master's that May. I felt free, and my stress melted away. My soul was joyful, and I would wake up in the middle of the night and wave my hands towards the heavens and whisper, "I love You so much, Lord." *Tears of faith.*

In June of 2022, I was able to resign from that financial institution and step into the next chapter of my life. I enjoy the calmness while I can. As an anointed daughter of God, I know He's been preparing me to fully walk in my destiny and I know it won't be a smooth walk. When God created us, He created us with purpose, and that purpose comes with a price–heartache, mistakes, challenges, and loneliness, however, the reward is putting a smile on God's face.

In 2023, I learned that the department where Lisa and Shelby had mistreated me was shut down, and they no longer held roles with direct reports. I often wonder if God used me to expose a longstanding systemic issue that needed to come to light. I never questioned His purpose, as it wasn't important to know why. What truly mattered was that I successfully completed the challenge He placed before me.

Where Do I Go From Here?

Developing my relationship with God has been an ongoing journey, one that deepens with each passing day. The first step was accepting that the Lord loves me unconditionally, with my faults and all–a realization that took years to embrace. He created me with love, purpose, and destiny. I'm unique, one of a kind, and in my heart, I believe I'm His favorite child.

For years, I struggled to look in the mirror and see myself as an image of God's love and creation, believing that no one could ever change that, not even me. Over time, I learned that my past doesn't define me. I'm a survivor because God created me for a greater purpose. He took that dark past and transformed it for His glory, allowing me to bring that darkness into the light to help others.

I created a prayer life out of desperation, loneliness, and hope, realizing God was my only lifeline. He has always known me and has never left my side, His mighty hand always reaching out for me to grasp. I began to read my Bible daily, and as I did, I began to ask God questions about His word. I wondered, "What was the purpose of creating women warriors who were brave yet tenderhearted?" and "How do I align with the biblical women who walked in faith?" I knew my battles were spiritual, but I questioned how many I would face in this earthly life.

Where do I go from here? The answer is simple–wherever God leads me. Whatever He asks me to do, I will do. Whatever He asks me to say, I will say. Will there be more trials, challenges, and tribulations? Absolutely! Will God walk with me, carry me when I'm weak, and never leave me or forsake me? Without a doubt! Will I continue to trust and praise Him until I get to heaven? Absolutely!

Will I shed more tears? Absolutely! Will I continue to praise Him through those tears? Absolutely! The Lord is compassionate and collects every tear we shed. When I hurt and cry out to my Heavenly Father, I believe He stops everything to comfort me because His love for me is immeasurable. When I praise Him from the depths of my soul and tears flow with joy and thanksgiving, I believe He smiles from His throne in Heaven, sharing my joy because He's delighted by my love for Him.

> **Heart Check-in**
>
> "He will again have compassion on us and will subdue our iniquities. You will cast all our sins into the depths of the sea." (Micah 7:19)
>
> Forgive yourself and let go of the past–God did.

Until next time, may the Lord shower you with strength, wisdom, determination, a pure heart, and a deep desire for a closer relationship with Him. May He fill you with a love that embraces all. Amen.

ABOUT THE AUTHOR

Sheila McDaniel was raised in Detroit, Michigan, where she made the life-changing decision to serve her country by joining the United States Air Force. She dedicated six years to her nation before moving to Rochester, New York, where she met her husband and relocated to California. It was in California that she began stepping boldly into her spiritual calling. When her marriage ended, Sheila moved to North Carolina, where she felt God calling her to draw closer to Him. There, she learned to trust Him fully and experienced healing from past wounds.

In 1993, Sheila gave her life to Christ, a decision that shaped her ever since. A passionate mentor, she guides and encourages teenage girls aged 13 to 17, sharing the Word of God through ministry, teaching, and prophecy. Sheila organizes and hosts women's conferences across the country, empowering and inspiring women of all ages. She is dedicated to serving others, whether it's feeding the homeless or spreading hope and encouragement. As an entrepreneur, speaker, and leader, Sheila is committed to living out her calling to help others through faith and love.

Sheila views education as a powerful tool for empowerment. In 2002, she was honored to serve as the commencement speaker when she earned both her Master of Computer Information Systems and Bachelor of Science in Business Information Systems from the University of Phoenix-Southern California Campus. Sheila also holds an associate degree in Electrical Engineering Technology from Monroe Community College and an undergraduate certificate in Cloud Computing from American Military University.

Professionally, Sheila has built an impressive career in Information Technology, excelling in roles such as Technical Program Project Lead, Scrum Master, IT Infrastructure Project Manager, and PMO leader. Her dedication, expertise, and leadership have earned her respect within the IT field.

At the core of Sheila's life is God and her family. She is a proud mother to two adult children and a grandmother, cherishing the joy and love they bring into her life. In her spare time, Sheila enjoys international travel, shopping, reading, dancing, exercising, and relaxing on the beach. She also loved the thrill of riding her Harley Davidson motorcycle. Recently, Sheila has embarked on a new creative venture as an author, working on her book *Tears of Faith*, which chronicles her spiritual journey.

Sheila McDaniel

Names of God Praise Song

I sing the Names of God as a praise song. I create a unique sound and dance almost every time I sing it. Customize the song and make it your own. The goal is to give God the praise.

You are **El Shaddai** – Lord God Almighty;
You are **El Elyon** – The Most High God;
You are **Adonai** – Lord, Master;
You are **Yahweh** – Lord, Jehovah;

You are **Jehovah Nissi** – The Lord My Banner;
You are **Jehovah Raah** – The Lord My Shepherd;
You are **Jehovah Rapha** – The Lord That Heals;
You are **Jehovah Shammah** – The Lord Is There;

You are **Jehovah Tsidkenu** – The Lord Our Righteousness;
You are **Jehovah Mekoddishkem** – The Lord Who Sanctifies You;
You are **El Olam** – The Everlasting God;
You are **Elohim** – God;

You are **Jehovah Jireh** – The Lord Will Provide;
You are ***Jehovah Shalom*** – The Lord Is Peace;
You are ***Jehovah Sabaoth*** – The Lord Of Host;
Amen, Amen, and Amen

www.ingramcontent.com/pod-product-compliance
Lightning Source LLC
Chambersburg PA
CBHW030451100526
44580CB00005B/80/J